1988

Landmarks of world literature

Leo Tolstoy

ANNA KARENINA

Landmarks of world literature

General Editor: J. P. Stern

LEO TOLSTOY

Anna Karenina

ANTHONY THORLBY

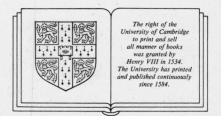

The right of the
University of Cambridge
to print and sell
all manner of books
was granted by
Henry VIII in 1534.
The University has printed
and published continuously
since 1584.

CAMBRIDGE UNIVERSITY PRESS

Cambridge
New York   New Rochelle   Melbourne   Sydney

Published by the Press Syndicate of the University of Cambridge
The Pitt Building, Trumpington Street, Cambridge CB2 1RP
32 East 57th Street, New York, NY 10022, USA
10 Stamford Road, Oakleigh, Melbourne 3166, Australia

First published 1987

Printed in Great Britain at
the University Press, Cambridge

British Library cataloguing in publication data

Thorlby, Anthony
Leo Tolstoy: Anna Karenina. − (Landmarks
of world literature).
1. Tolstoi, L.N. − Lev Nikolaevich. Anna
Karenina
I. Title   II. Series
891.73′3   PG3365.A6

Library of Congress cataloguing in publication data

Thorlby, Anthony.
Leo Tolstoy, Anna Karenina.
(Landmarks of world literature)
Bibliography.
1. Tolstoy, Leo, graf, 1828–1910. Anna Karenina.
I. Title.   II. Series.
PG3365.A63T48   1987   891.73′3   87–15167

ISBN 0 521 32819 5 hard covers
ISBN 0 521 31325 2 paperback

Contents

v

Chronology

	Tolstoy's life and publications	Major literary events	Important historical events
1828	28 August (old style, 9 September new style) Lev Nikolayevich Tolstoy born at Yasnaya Polyana, 200 km S.W. of Moscow		
1830	Mother dies	Stendhal's *The Red and the Black*	Louis Philippe constitutional king of France
1832			Constitutional monarchy in Belgium, Reform Bill in Britain
1847	Inherits Yasnaya with serfs		
1848			Abortive revolutions in Europe
1850		Tennyson's 'In Memoriam' Wagner's *Lohengrin*	
1851	Goes with brother Nikolay Tolstoy to Caucasus; serves as a volunteer in the army; writes *Childhood*		Crystal Palace Exhibition *Coup d'état* of Louis Napoleon
1852		Thackeray's *Henry Esmond*	
1852–3	Campaigns in Caucasus; writes *Boyhood*; starts *The Cossacks*	Dickens's *Bleak House*	
1854–5	Receives commission; serves at Sevastopol; writes *Sevastopol Sketches* and *Youth*		Outbreak of Crimean War
1856	Death of Dmitry Tolstoy; *Two Hussars*		
1856–7		Flaubert's *Madame Bovary*	

Date	Tolstoy's life		Historical events
1857	Travels in France, Germany, Switzerland	Baudelaire's *Les Fleurs du mal*; Trollope's *Barchester Towers*	
1857–67		Herzen's 'The Bell'	
1859	Establishes a school at Yasnaya Polyana	Darwin's *Origin of Species*	
1860–1	Visits Germany, France, Italy, England, and Belgium; Death of Nikolay Tolstoy at Hyères (October 1860)		
1861	Quarrel with Turgenev		Emancipation of the serfs in Russia; United Kingdom of Italy proclaimed
1861–2	Briefly a local magistrate		
1861–5			American Civil War
1862	Police search Yasnaya Polyana. Marries Sofya Andreyevna Behrs; Shuts school	Turgenev's *Fathers and Children*; Hugo's *Les Misérables*	
1863–9	At Yasnaya; visits to Moscow; Writes *War and Peace*		
1864		Goncourt's *Germaine Lacerteux*	The First International
1866		Dostoyevsky's *Crime and Punishment*	
1867		Ibsen's *Peer Gynt*; Zola's *Thérèse Raquin*	
1869–71	Studies Schopenhauer, Greek		
1870			
1871	Bad health; *kumys* cure in Samara.		Prussia defeats France
1871–2		Eliot's *Middlemarch*	Paris Commune

1872	Reopens school, writes *ABC Book*	
1873–7	Writes *Anna Karenina*	
1878	Moral crisis and conversion to a non-supernatural Christianity	
1879	Writes *A Confession*	
1879–80		Dostoyevsky's *The Brothers Karamazov*
		Meredith's *The Egoist*
1879–83	Theological studies	
1881	Appeals to Tsar to pardon assassins of Alexander II	Tsar Alexander II assassinated
1883	Writes *What I Believe*	Ibsen's *Ghosts*
1884	*What I Believe* banned	Verga's *I Malavoglia*
1885	Founds *The Intermediary* to supply reading matter for peasants; writes parable stories, 'Ivan the Fool', 'Two Old Men', 'Does a Man Need Much Earth?'	Nietzsche's *Thus Spake Zarathustra* Huysmans's *A Rebours* Zola's *Germinal*
1886	*What Then Must We Do? Death of Ivan Ilyich* (story)	Hardy's *The Mayor of Casterbridge*
1886–7		Galdos's *Fortunata y Jacinta*
1887	*On Life*, Tolstoyan communities formed	Strindberg's *The Father* 1887, 1897 Jubilees of Queen Victoria
1888		Strindberg's *Miss Julie*
1889	*The Kreutzer Sonata* (story)	Fabian Essays in Socialism

1891	Renounces his copyrights and divides property among family	Hardy's *Tess of the d'Urbervilles*	
1891–2	Undertakes famine relief		
1893	*The Kingdom of God is Within You*		
1894	*Christianity and Patriotism, Reason and Religion, Religion and Morality*	Kipling's *The Jungle Book* D'Annunzio's *The Triumph of Death*	
1894– 1904			Dreyfus Affair in France
1895	Death of son Ivan. Appeals for Dukhobors	Wilde's *The Importance of Being Ernest*	
1896	*Master and man* (story) *How to Read the Gospels*	Fontane's *Effi Briest* Chekhov's *The Seagull* Proust's *Les Plaisirs et les jours*	
1898	*What is Art?*		
1899	Finishes novel, *Resurrection*		
1900	*The Slavery of our Times*		
1901	Virtual excommunication by Holy Synod, *Reply to the Synod's Edict*; illness; taken to Yalta	Mann's *Buddenbrooks*	
1902	*What is Religion?*	Gorky's *The Lower Depths* Conrad's *Youth* ('Heart of Darkness')	
1903		James's *The Ambassadors*	
1904	*Bethink Yourselves!* (against war)		Outbreak of Russo-Japanese War

1905	Alyosha the Pot; Fyodor Kuzmich (stories)	Forster's Where Angels Fear to Tread	Strikes, revolutionary ferment in Russia; elected legislature (Duma)
1908	I Cannot Be Silent! (against hangings of revolutionaries).		
1909	Growing quarrels with wife Corresponds with Ghandi		
1910	Leaves home; dies at Astapovo railway station		

Note on translations

Passages from *Anna Karenina* have generally been quoted from the Penguin edition, translated by Rosemary Edmonds, 1954; in a few instances a new translation is given. Passages from Tolstoy's Letters and Diaries are taken from the two-volume editions by Professor R. F. Christian, 1978 and 1985. Passages from Russian critics in Chapter 3 are quoted from A. V. Knowles, *Tolstoy, The Critical Heritage*, 1978.

Chapter 1

Background to *Anna Karenina*

When Tolstoy began work, in March 1873, on the novel which he eventually called *Anna Karenina*, he already had behind him the massive achievement of *War and Peace*. Although it had stirred up much controversy and criticism, that vast epic of Russian life with its grand patriotic theme from the nation's history had revealed its author's incomparable powers, and great things were now expected of him, not least by himself. It was not an easy situation in which to find his way to a new subject, but Tolstoy's development never had been smooth, nor ever would be in the future; soul-searching and intellectual struggle were the stuff of his existence. He had always been something of a maverick amongst the writers of his generation, with many of whom he quarrelled — with Turgenev so bitterly that there was talk of a duel. Most had been more than ready to acknowledge him; he had early shown that he could write a new kind of realistic narrative, closely modelled on actual experiences of his own, amongst the family, in the Caucasus, at Sevastopol, which was distinctively original and vivid. It had all the imaginative life of fiction with none of the contrivance or artifice. But then his production had faltered. Tolstoy's conscience was troubled by many concerns besides literary ones: by personal moral failings, by religious and philosophical doubts, above all by the big social problems of backward Russia in his day. His contemporaries were as disturbed by these as he was, of course, but he never could ally himself for long with any party of the intelligentsia: mainly perhaps because he was never content merely to write about the problems which concerned him. More than once he considered giving up work as a writer, and part of his quarrel with Turgenev was due to his impatience with a purely literary and aesthetic attitude to life.

1

But if Tolstoy could not agree with the aesthetes, nor could he agree with the radicals, that literature should be used for political ends — he even wrote some not very successful stories in defence of art. But what was art, and what ought it to be, if art for art's sake was morally unacceptable? This profoundly serious question was never far from his mind; it led him in the end to write his challenging tract *What Is Art?* and to the conviction that his own earlier work, including *War and Peace* and *Anna Karenina*, was worthless. In the meanwhile, his passionate obsession with the moral meaning of life, both in reality and in imagination, surely helped to form his unusually intense style of realism.

The last volume of *War and Peace* was published in December 1869; it sold out as quickly as the earlier volumes had done two years before, and it revived the critical dispute which had gone on in the years between. Few questioned Tolstoy's artistry, except with regard to the view of the world it conveyed, and this provoked many conflicting opinions; it has done so ever since. Disagreement focuses on Tolstoy's idea of history, both as he expresses it directly in theoretical passages in the novel, and as it implicitly and much more persuasively appears in his depiction of characters, especially historical ones, and of events; even personal and quite fictitious experiences are inevitably coloured by it. Remembering what he had seen at Sevastopol, Tolstoy contrasts the reality of individual soldiers' courage and suffering with the delusions of vain and corrupt generals, particularly Napoleon; the Russians in 1812 are shown to have been sustained not by superior generalship but by their unconscious will as a people. Doubtless the theory has flaws, but the events depicted appear more powerfully lifelike, rather than less, as a result of not being explained in conventional historical terms. Tolstoy was inspired by an unusually strong mixture of philosophical reflection, much of it directed against the positivism prevalent at the time he was writing, and of imaginative feeling for the physical and subjective immediacy of experience. It is absurd to wish, as some critics have done, that he had been less inclined to philosophize; it is precisely the combined strength of both impulses in him, the intellectual and the sensuous, the passionate and the reflective, each of them in its way religious though not orthodox, that enables him to conceive scenes which represent so memorably the situation of individuals both within history and outside it, leading both a life of their own and the life of all. To understand the truth of his situation, about which Tolstoy never ceased to agonize, a man must be mindful of the timeless and natural relationships in which he stands, mindful of love and family, God and nature; he must not allow himself to be swept away by the passing pressures of history. History is a snare and a delusion, and human attempts to govern it are worse than futile. And this every peasant intuitively knows; so at least Tolstoy wanted to believe, for he idealized the spiritual condition of the Russian *muzhik*, preserved by ignorance from the taint of civilization.

Not surprisingly, Tolstoy's contemporaries had difficulty in placing him. His belief in man's natural goodness and freedom, which he derived from Rousseau, his antagonism towards the state and his sympathy with the peasants all suggested that he must be a radical. Had not the village schools he set up been suspected of subversion and raided by the police? However, it was not revolution that was being taught there, but something rather more like what would now be called child-centred learning. Although Tolstoy was 'going to the people' in the manner urged by the revolutionary, Herzen, and advocated — rather more often than attempted — by a whole generation of intellectuals in Russia who called themselves Slavophiles and Populists, he was never their close ally. He was opposed to violence, and had no desire to institute republican or any other form of government. If he subscribed in effect to a kind of anarchism, it was quite unlike Bakunin's, for he aspired to reform the existing order spiritually and peacefully, rather than to build on its ruins. Above all, he could not accept the materialism of many of these radicals and nihilists; all his life he was preoccupied with moral happiness and the welfare of the soul, especially his own, and he suspected the body of leading men astray. In later years, as he grew to denounce sexuality and material possessions ever more strongly, it became apparent that his doctrine was one of saintliness rather than socialism. His international reputation enabled him to be exceptionally outspoken on social and even political matters, but he was not so much aiding the revolutionary cause as competing with it; some of his ends might look similar, but his means did not, while his attitude towards history and science were plainly unprogressive. And there were other reasons, of temperament, of heredity perhaps, and of class, why Tolstoy stood apart. He was an aristocrat with a profound sense of tradition, the inheritor of an ancient title and of the great estate where he had been born; the thousands of acres of Yasnaya Polyana came to him together with over three hundred male serfs and their families. His efforts at educating his people were laudable, no doubt, but he never questioned his right to teach them as he wished; when he grew tired of his schools, he simply closed them. He not only refused to enter government service, on principle; he had no conception of organized cooperation with others for political or administrative ends. Like his hero, Levin, he could see no sense in the attempts at local government in the countryside by means of the *zemstvos* (district councils). His intense urge towards freedom, which was one of the strongest traits of his nature, expressed an innate sense of personal independence, rather than a shared, civic ideal. The intelligentsia were alien to him partly because they lacked his roots in property and the soil. His dislike of the growing bourgeoisie and its capitalistic enterprise was in part the reaction of an old landowner to the forces of economic and industrial change. Levin's hostility towards Ryabinin, the speculator in land, is Tolstoy's own, and so are his aristocratic sentiments:

I consider myself and people like me aristocrats, people who can point back to three or four honourable generations, all with the highest degree of breeding (talent and intelligence are a different matter), who have never curried favour with anyone, never depended on anyone, but have lived like my father and grandfather before him.   (II, 17)

After the huge labour of finishing and publishing *War and Peace*, Tolstoy began reading widely and intensively. He studied Greek, in order to read Homer and Herodotus, he reread the plays of Shakespeare, Molière, and Goethe, but first of all he renewed his study of German philosophy, especially Schopenhauer. 'Do you know what this summer has meant for me?', he wrote in a letter, 'Constant raptures over Schopenhauer, a series of spiritual joys such as I have never known before' (30 Aug. 1869). Schopenhauer's philosophical pessimism confirmed, and may already have helped to form, Tolstoy's scepticism regarding history and science, as well as his mistrust of sexuality. More positively, something in Schopenhauer's imaginative sense of life corresponded deeply to his own. He also sensed the presence in life − in nature, in human beings, in experience − of a reality that no rational explanation can reach. Schopenhauer called it the Will to Life, and it dwarfed the mind. At the same time, Schopenhauer taught, each individual enjoys intimate awareness of this vital mystery, for it exists in him, it is what he truly is, it constitutes that aspect of his being which is most intimately himself, his individuality. Tolstoy's feeling for individual character and experience, especially in its subjective essence, was strong, and it was precisely individuation which Schopenhauer made into the metaphysical principle and goal of existence. The variety and vitality of Tolstoy's characterizations can no more be reduced, of course, to a single philosophical idea than can people in real life; they are unique creations not philosophical concepts. But some of Schopenhauer's concepts do make it possible to grasp distinctive features of human beings, in Tolstoy's fiction and in life: a core of irreducible and forceful identity, a quality of sheer selfhood, a *samodovol'nost* expressing itself sometimes as complacent self-assurance. In his enthusiasm for Schopenhauer, Tolstoy may also have become aware of a very pronounced trait in his own character; his wife noted once in her diary: 'Sometimes his assurance and his self-possession annoy me' (31 July 1868).

Similarly, Schopenhauer's meditations on death clearly correspond to but did not cause Tolstoy's own recurrent, highly personal obsession with death. This dates back at least to the time when his brother Dmitry had died in harrowing circumstances which he never forgot (he recreates them and Dmitry in *Anna Karenina* in a scene filled with memories also of the death of another brother, Nikolay, also from tuberculosis). Tolstoy was liable ever afterwards to suffer attacks of sudden, visionary despair at the inevitability and closeness of death; one such occurred in this same summer of 1869. His very vital, strongly physical sense of personal identity and his vivid imaginative horror at the prospect of personal annihilation are evidently complementary aspects of the same mind, if not of the same philosophy. Both enter his writing, where they provide one of the basic contrasts out of which he composes his picture of the real. Anna Karenina is irritated by the *samodovol'nost* of her lover and fights it to the death. And 'Death' is the only title to be given to any chapter in the novel: the one in which Levin's brother, who is called Nikolay, dies of tuberculosis.

Tolstoy pours out much of his own experience through the character of Levin — whose name echoes his own first name: Lev — including his philosophical and religious doubts, his moral crises, and his suicidal despair. Years later, in his *Confession*, he describes himself in the same words he uses of Levin: 'Then I, the happy man, removed the rope from my room . . . and stopped taking my gun when I went out to hunt, so that I could not yield too easily to the desire to do away with myself.' He also endows Levin with his own love of the country, dislike of society, idealization of the peasants and of manual work, and with ideas for better and fairer management of the land. When Levin goes hunting, his enjoyment is Tolstoy's. Even more remarkably, Levin's experiences of betrothal and marriage are also Tolstoy's own, down to such details as the difference in age between himself and his young bride, their exchange of intimacies by means of the first letters of words written on a table in chalk, his insistence on showing her his diaries and her shock at his sexual confessions, the crisis of doubt at the last minute, the delay at the wedding owing to wrongly packed shirts; and the list goes on through many details of married life, including domestic irritations and misunderstandings, and the dramatic dismissal from the house of a bachelor guest who appeared to Tolstoy too assiduous in his attentions to his wife, Sonya. The fact that so many details of this kind are autobiographical does not, of course, lend them any greater interest or effectiveness in the novel; what is noteworthy is rather that they are not any less effectively imagined, and that material of this kind forms a seamless whole with invented matter. This ability to blend factual with fictitious narrative, to realize the imaginary and imagine the real as though there were no difference between them, to cast real life and fiction in the same mould, that is surely the hallmark of Tolstoy's genius.

The idea for a novel about a woman of society guilty of adultery occurred to Tolstoy already in February, 1870. According to a diary note made by his wife, the problem for Tolstoy was 'to make the woman pitiable but not contemptible; when this creature came into his mind as a type, all the masculine characters he had previously invented immediately grouped themselves around her' (23 Feb. 1870). At the time, however, he was preoccupied with a quite different subject: he planned to write another big historical novel, set in the period of Peter the Great. He read more and more history books, took endless notes, but after three years had still not started. 'I have now reached the point in my research at which I am beginning to go round in circles', he declared in a letter (24 Jan. 1873). In March of that year he made repeated attempts to begin the book and failed, and then he suddenly turned to something else: 'A novel on contemporary life', Sonya wrote to her sister. 'The subject is the unfaithful wife and all the ensuing tragedy' (19 Mar. 1873). The release of his creative powers was immediate, suggesting that he had simply been pushing himself in the wrong direction. Only eight weeks later he wrote to Strakhov, his close literary friend and most admiring critic: 'I am writing a novel that has nothing to do with Peter the Great; I started it over a month ago and have finished it in draft form. This novel — I mean a novel, the first in my life — is very close to my heart, and I am

completely wrapped up in it' (11 May 1873). The remark
(about this being the 'first novel' in his life) may seem surprising, coming from the author of *War and Peace*; that had
evidently not been a novel in Tolstoy's mind. A number of
other comments in the same vein — for instance, in a draft
introduction and in 'A Few Words about the Book *War and
Peace*' — suggest that Tolstoy considered that a true novel
ought to have a single plot ending in a *dénouement*, and also
that the novel form was European rather than Russian.

What had caused this change of heart and given Tolstoy
this new impetus? Partly the realization that he had 'nothing
in common' with the people of Peter the Great's time, and
that his moral and religious concerns were very much with
and of the present — he was disturbed, for instance, by the
freer attitudes towards sex and marriage which were developing in the sixties and seventies. While he was still wrestling
with his historical material, we find him much impressed by
a recent book upholding a husband's duty to discipline and
punish, even kill, an unfaithful wife (this work, *L'Homme-
Femme*, was written by Alexandre Dumas *fils*, who included
an instance of such fatal punishment in a play the following
year). Then there was a tragic occurrence which had affected
him deeply the previous year; the mistress of a neighbour,
deserted by her lover for another woman, had committed
suicide by throwing herself under a train at a nearby station.
Tolstoy had attended the inquest; the woman's name had
been Anna. Finally, there was Pushkin: by chance Tolstoy
reread the *Tales of Belkin* ('for the seventh time, I think'),
and was particularly impressed by the fragment beginning,
'The guests were arriving at the country house'. That was the
way to begin, right in the middle of the action. 'Involuntarily,
unwittingly, not knowing why and what would come of it, I
thought up characters and events, began to go on with it, then
of course changed it, and suddenly all the threads became so
well and truly tied up that the result was a novel' (25 Mar.
1873). The similarity of Tolstoy's first sentence to Pushkin's
is apparent: 'After the opera, the guests reassembled at the
home of the young Countess Vraski'; somewhat modified this

became eventually the first sentence of chapter 6 of Part II.

The novel took much longer to complete than Tolstoy had expected, and his first flush of creative enthusiasm was not sustained. Moods of doubt returned about the value of writing at all, and especially writing literature of this sort. His son Ilya reports him as having said of the novel: 'What's so difficult about describing how an officer gets entangled with a woman? There's nothing difficult about that, and above all, nothing worthwhile. It's bad and it serves no purpose.' When the first part was finished, in March 1874, and was being prepared for serial publication in *The Russian Herald*, Tolstoy had already lost interest and wanted to get back to teaching his peasant children: 'I simply cannot tear myself away from living beings to bother with imaginary ones', he wrote (?Dec. 1874). Other factors depressed him: The death of three of his infant children, the prolonged illness of Sonya, worn out by pregnancies and grief, the loss of two dearly loved aunts. He began to feel that his powers were weakening, and wrote to Strakhov: 'If only someone else could finish *Anna Karenina* for me' (8 Nov. 1875). In the autumn of 1876 his energy returned and Sonya, returned to health, was performing her amazing feats as a copyist. When the proofs came, Tolstoy covered them with so many revisions that they were indecipherable except to her, and she had to make fair copies. The public − though by no means all the critics − grew evermore enthusiastic about each new instalment, and Tolstoy purported to be amazed: 'The success of the last section [VII] of *Anna Karenina* pleased me greatly, I must confess. It was so unexpected: I am astonished to see that something as ordinary and insignificant as that can please the public' (26 Jan. 1877). When Strakhov sent him two laudatory reviews, Tolstoy burned them − to test his own moral integrity. He soon got an even better opportunity to prove his moral fibre. While he was writing the Epilogue (Part VIII), news came of the uprising of the Serbs and Montenegrins against the Turks, and in April 1877 Russia declared war on Turkey. By then Tolstoy had expressed through Levin pacifist views of the kind for which he was in later years to become internationally famous. *The Russian Herald* demanded revision of the now unpatriotic passages; Tolstoy refused to compromise, and decided to publish the Epilogue as a separate booklet, which appeared in January 1878. As he had foreseen, he was denounced for his lack of patriotic feeling — by Dostoyevsky, amongst others.

Throughout the summer of 1877, Strakhov helped Tolstoy prepare the first edition of *Anna Karenina* in book form, which appeared in January 1888. Strakhov's occasional timid criticisms may have been responsible for a few changes and deletions; but for the most part, as he later reported, he found that 'Lev Nikolayevich would defend his choice of words to the death, and refused to make the slightest alteration. I could see from his remarks that he cared a great deal about what he had written, and that, in spite of the seeming carelessness and awkwardness of his style, he had weighed every word and phrase as carefully as the most exacting poet' (*Reminiscences*).

Chapter 2

The novel

The stories and their theme

The reader of *Anna Karenina* soon discovers that he is being told not one story but two, and that, as the novel progresses, these two stories go quite separate ways. Even more remarkable is the fact that the novel's heroine, Anna, appears in only one of these stories, while the novel's hero, Levin, appears only in the other; they meet once, in a scene of seemingly no great consequence. If singleness of plot and *dénouement* are as fundamental to a novel as Tolstoy apparently believed, then he has once again written a rather different kind of narrative, though not as strikingly so as in *War and Peace*. The title leads us to expect that this will be essentially Anna's story, and though half of the book does not treat of her at all, her death does finally determine the novel's ending, after which the second story too is quickly drawn to a close. We find also that the two plots have been woven together here and there, and, even where they merely stand side by side or alternate, we sense that they are contributing to one another in important ways. So what is the reason for their combined presence in the novel, and what is their combined effect? Did something in Anna's story inspire the seemingly quite separate story of Levin? May the development of Levin's story have helped to make possible the full realization of Anna's tragic fate?

The personal separateness of Anna and Levin marks a fundamental difference between the social worlds they each inhabit. It is in the first place a difference of location. Anna lives in 'the top circle of Petersburg society', where her husband's official position in the Imperial administration, together with her own beauty, give her the entrée into its three most influential sets: that of senior officials, that of rather affectedly pious women and ambitiously intellectual men known as 'the conscience of Petersburg', and that of 'society proper — the world of balls, dinner-parties, brilliant toilettes, which clung onto the Court with one hand, lest it sink to the level of the demi-monde which the members of that fashionable world pretended to despise, though their tastes were not only similar but identical' (II, 4). Levin, by contrast, lives in the country, where he devotes himself to the farming of his estate; he does not go to the capital, and when he has occasion to be in town, the town is Moscow, whose society is more family-based and patrician. The way of government, the way of thinking, and the way of life represented by Petersburg, and to some extent even by Moscow also, are anathema to him. He is happiest working with peasants in the fields, or when he is out hunting; he has no town house nor any desire for a situation of elegance and public esteem, but wants his home to be a place of domesticity and private happiness. He is not concerned with social appearances or with career, the two dominant considerations in Anna's world, where typical scenes occur at the theatre and the races, which are essentially occasions of show and prestige. Levin's attention is absorbed by the appearances of earth and sky, and by the natural and necessary tasks of working the land; the fundamental physical reality of these makes the paper-work and politics of administration — not to mention the idle pursuits of the rich, and their salon-bred conversation — seem quite artificial. On that reality Levin takes his stand; it is the ground of his integrity, his touchstone in his struggle to place his life on a sure foundation of truth. It is also the ground on which his role as hero is based. For, although Tolstoy gives him such space and place in the novel as will attract the reader's attention to him as hero, he does not give him much in the way of plot. In fact, some events in his story, such as it is, show him in a rather humorous, even absurd light, as though Tolstoy wished to emphasize again in this way that he stands for a very different set of values from those which make the adventures in Anna's story so fatally serious. The seriousness of Levin's story is of a more un-worldly and philosophic kind.

To notice this separation of interest in *Anna Karenina* is to begin to wonder how Tolstoy has contrived to bind his im-mensely diverse material together. He does so firstly by link-ing the stories themselves at one or two points, most obvious-ly at the beginning. Love, marriage, and family provide the links, as they so often do in realist novels of the nineteenth century. Tolstoy introduces two families, whose affairs link the story of Anna with that of Levin, apart from developing some interest of their own as a kind of intermittent sub-plot. They are the Oblonskys and the Shcherbatskys, and through them Levin's bride, Kitty Shcherbatsky, finds herself for a while in the role of a defeated, jealous rival to Anna, while Anna's lover, Vronsky, seems to stand in the way of Levin. This rivalry leads to no external conflicts nor even, after one unhappy scene at a ball, to any significant contact; it is passively felt by Kitty and Levin, confined to their minds and feelings, where it is something to be overcome inwardly, through that quiet process of moral growth which brings them to discover themselves and their true love for one another.

There is, besides this connection, another one that pro-duces even less direct interaction between the story of Anna and Vronsky and that of Levin and Kitty. Anna is the sister of Stiva Oblonsky, and his wife, Dolly, is the sister of Kitty. Oblonsky is the novel's middleman, and he is wonderfully well portrayed: a genial, popular, pleasure-seeking man of the world, whom Tolstoy makes good use of to bring about meetings and help along the plot. Stiva is convinced that 'things will turn out all right', and that 'there is always a way out of every situation'. He is the kind of person who believes, so to speak, that life is a matter largely of plot; he is always engaged in some love-intrigue of his own, always trying to make the right arrangements, always confident that things can be steered towards a satisfactory conclusion. In this belief Tolstoy shows him to be very evidently mistaken, though doubtless nothing would ever cause him to change it. Stiva's significance for the novel is only partly to act as the busybody of the plot; it is partly also to let it be seen that there is in life much more than can be arranged and patched up. His own family situation reflects in a much more commonplace, less heroic light aspects of both the two main stories: like his sister, Anna, he too is guilty of marital infidelity. His wife Dolly, on the other hand, like her sister in turn, has the capacity and the desire to be fully absorbed by her family and children. 'It runs in the family', as another of the Shcherbatsky sisters says. Tolstoy even causes the differences in location and life-style between Anna's story and Levin's to be reflected also in the Oblonsky household, which is seen both enmeshed in the vanities of city society, and also secure in the contentment of country living.

Tolstoy does not introduce and dwell upon these family relationships merely because they are useful for his plot. Family life was always a subject apt to stir his imagination most deeply. His earliest works, *Childhood, Boyhood*, and *Youth*, are semi-autobiographical; they show already the kind of writing he would always be good at and how much he owes to his sense of homely realities. In his personal life, especially during the years when he wished to marry and in the happier periods of his marriage, Tolstoy cherished a high ideal of family. It was much more in his eyes than a merely social institution, let alone a social convenience. It had an imaginative significance that was coloured for him by many moral and religious considerations. The situation of the individual within the family, and especially the situation which brings two individuals together to found a family, were for him the earliest and happiest experience of man's place in the natural order; they were touched therefore by Tolstoy's wealth of feeling for that order, which had near mystical overtones. His view of family is consequently never narrowly moralistic nor tritely sentimental, and it is relatively unconcerned with questions of money; inevitably it calls to mind Tolstoy's social circumstances, unusual by European standards, as an aristocrat and landowner in rural Russia, which helped to foster, while not necessitating, his distinctive idealism. His idealistic hopes and beliefs with regard to family life illumine much of his writing, not only in such an obvious expression of them as *Family Happiness*, but more memorably in the epilogue to *War and Peace*.

In *Anna Karenina*, Tolstoy alerts us to the importance of this theme with his opening sentence: no sooner has the title of the book led us to expect one woman's story than we are asked to think about something rather different: the happiness of families and the differences between them. The heroine's story alone does not hold this novel together, as we have seen; to do this, Tolstoy relies on the moral and thematic interest of family life. It is this which provides the most obvious connection between the two separate love stories, even where there is otherwise no actual narrative link. Anna's love story is, from this thematic point of view, just as much a family story as Levin's, despite the fact that hers ends in disaster, whereas his ends in happiness. The shape and progress of the two stories match one another: in the first half of the novel, the lives of the lovers are not yet united, while in the second half they are. This is the case not only with Levin and Kitty but also with Anna and Vronsky, whose love affair is regarded for a long while as secret, albeit a very open one. Tolstoy shows them together in remarkably few scenes, and in these they talk of their desire to 'unite their lives' and live as man and wife. For both couples transition from life apart to life together occurs at the same moment and in closely connected circumstances. It is at Oblonsky's dinner party that Levin and Kitty finally confess their love for one another, while — for no other reason than that of thematic structure — Karenin is there too, meditating the divorce to which his agreement will be crucial in allowing Anna and Vronsky to join their lives. In both cases the transition is sudden and overwhelming, the acknowledgement of a state of heart which has long existed, and the realisation of a thematic truth, which the reader by now feels to be right and necessary. The direction and meaning of love lie in a shared life together, a joint presence in society; the promise of inner and private feeling demands fulfilment in the open and public sphere of home and family. Tolstoy makes this transformation seem particularly momentous by introducing into each story dramatic delays and spiritual upheavals, crises of doubt, abandonment of everything, which bring Anna and Vronsky to their death-beds — at least, they expect and wish to die. But they do not; their story is not allowed to end at this romantic climax. The more testing experience of married life awaits them, and its demands are for Tolstoy more inexorably grounded in the necessary order of things than the hazards of purely individual romance.

It is doubtless obvious enough that the thematic interest which arises from the juxtaposition of these two stories, and from the contrasts and parallels it suggests to the reader, is of a broadly moral kind, reflecting Tolstoy's ideal of married life. It is not at all obvious whether the great mass of varied and beautifully lifelike material which the novel brings together in this way is only or even primarily of moral interest. Traditional criticism used always to be aware, of course, that whatever moral or other kind of instruction a work of literature contains, it also contains a good deal of purely imaginative interest besides, which was then rather aptly called pleasure. The disadvantage of this approach was that it made the two kinds of interest sound rather too distinct from one another. More recent criticism has simply abandoned the question, by dismissing literature's ability to instruct at all; this tends to leave little to take pleasure in either, except perhaps in seeing how artificial and untrue literature's images are. Suspicion that any view of reality may be arbitrary permits only one true conviction; that truth itself is literally unimaginable. Tolstoy's moral realism, by contrast, is untouched by such doubts; if they are characteristic of modern styles of writing, then his own is not yet modern. He could imagine truth very well. His exceptionally powerful imagination and his scarcely less powerful sense of moral concern combine to produce a text in which imaginative interest and moral interest are not only both palpably present, but also interact and modify one another. What Tolstoy imagines to be real is considerably influenced by what he believes to be moral, and what he believes to be moral is influenced by what he imagines to be real. His realism is all of one piece with his moral conviction, so that he rarely moralizes directly by making moral pronouncements about what is going on in the narrative from some position of his own outside it. Indeed, we do not have the feeling, as we read, that life is being arraigned before moral principles distinct from itself, either in our mind or in Tolstoy's; and this could lead us to wonder in what sense moral judgement can still be appropriate when it appears that everything in life has to be the way it is. For the moment let us say simply that Tolstoy makes the realization of moral truth look identical with the process itself of life, and conclude that the thematic unity and interest of the novel also lie in the discovery of this process.

The importance of moral contrast as a source of imaginative inspiration for Tolstoy will be familiar to a reader coming to *Anna Karenina* from *War and Peace*, where an even greater range of material was similarly composed around the broad moral opposition indicated by the title. And early drafts of *Anna Karenina*, too, show that Tolstoy immediately thought of his new theme, that of 'the unfaithful wife', once again in terms of contrasts, which were to arise from the stories of *Two Marriages* or *Two Couples*, as he provisionally entitled the novel. At this stage, the family contrasting with the Karenins were the Oblonskys; Levin was barely present. Vronsky looked like becoming the figure of chief intellectual interest, being much more intelligent than Anna, who was herself a less attractive person, sexually coquettish and patently blameworthy. With the development of Levin, this pattern of contrasts was entirely changed, and with it the moral structure and conception of the book. The impression is strong that it was, so to speak, thanks to Levin that Tolstoy found himself able to develop Anna into the altogether more positive and attractive heroine we now have: beautiful, charming, capable of great tenderness and love, and endowed with a spiritual seriousness, honesty, and integrity equal to Levin's own. With Levin providing a more ideal point of reference than anything to be found within fashionable society, the conflict and contrast between Anna and all those around her, including her husband, could be represented in her favour. Tolstoy gradually dared, in fact, to explore the force of sexual passion in its most winning guise, where everything seems to speak for it: beauty and charm and vitality and a kind of natural moral justification. It was a force to which he was himself very susceptible; the sensuousness of his imagination is its spontaneous ally, and he writes as though he were in love with his heroine. What could contain such passion? It was easy enough to deal with frivolous and merely physical infatuation; but what of a great love that is also illicit? Tolstoy's solution was to find moral ground firm enough to allow him to accept imaginatively the fullest and finest appeal of such passion, and then convincingly to reject it and portray its destruction. And it is through Levin that he establishes this ground. Not all readers find Levin and his views sufficiently interesting or persuasive; they think them irrelevant to the main story. The problem is similar to that raised by Tolstoy's views on history which he needed in *War and Peace*, more than some critics have wished to accept, in order to contain the ravages of war. Whatever Tolstoy's success there in integrating his moral and his imaginative vision, it will be argued here that each is indispensable to the other.

To some readers nowadays, of course, it looks as though Anna is made to suffer solely on account of hypocritical social prejudices, which Tolstoy both exposes and then cruelly allows to prevail. D. H. Lawrence, for one, considered that Tolstoy had betrayed the relationship of Anna and Vronsky, whose passion promised more than he allowed to be fulfilled. Tolstoy, however, understood both love and personal fulfilment in less narrowly sexual terms than Lawrence; his broader moral vision embraces much else besides — the needs of family and of each of the sexes, the need for work and for some social community, the need above all to confront life's spiritual challenge, and ultimately death, with comprehending faith. It is to the reality of these needs that Levin continuously bears witness; his story is one of inner struggle to satisfy and harmonize them. This reality, rather than Levin in his person alone or in particular ideas or actions of his, provides the dimension of moral contrast in the novel. A kind of realism results, which is remarkable for much more than the extra slice of life in the country that Levin brings with him. Through his story points of moral reference are established, which are valid for the novel as a whole. The perspective of understanding which allowed Tolstoy to endow Anna with such tremendous appeal leaves her with no escape from a tragic end. We come to see how the circumstances of her passion render it profoundly, almost demoniacally intense; the lovers' very ardour arises from their social situation, from their focus on themselves, their dependence on their feelings, their inability to compromise. With how much else besides is Levin concerned! In a world where the parameters of his experience are the true ones, the downfall of Anna's relationship with Vronsky is not only morally comprehensible but tragically inevitable.

To argue that the unifying thematic interest in *Anna Karenina* has moral significance, that it also contributes to the structure of Tolstoy's realism, and then in addition that it enables him to achieve a truly tragic ending is to make large claims for its importance. We are not dealing with separate components of his style, of course, for all that these critical concepts tend to pull in different directions. Realism in fiction, and to some extent the novel form generally, is not readily associated with tragedy, for reasons resting on the fundamental dissimilarity of the two literary genres. The first cause of tragedy is a doom that cannot be averted, the so-called tragic inevitability of its story, which begins with high expectation of something better – as Anna's does, in fact. The reason why tragic effect is difficult to achieve in fiction is that a novelist appears to be in a position to control everything and explain anything. If things go badly, it is hard for him to represent this as a fate beyond his or his characters' control; he or they will appear responsible. This is because the management of the story lies in his hands, his voice can be heard in every event and description, he knows what each of the characters inwardly thinks and feels and whatever else he pleases outside their ken; above all he has it in his power to make the reader privy to a kind of universal knowledge of what exists in the world — within individuals, and quite apart from them in the world at large. How sharply delineated and restricted is the dramatist's scope for expression, by comparison, and how much less are we as spectators told. We can only watch the actors bringing their own story about, as helpless as they; reality is confined to what a small group can do and say in a situation no bigger than a stage and no longer than an hour or two. It is these limits which make possible the impression of inescapability, in a close sequence of quite brief moments of action, with attention focused on bare exchanges of words, as though nothing else in the world existed or were even possible. Where is the novelist to find any such vocabulary of necessity? Necessity lies in the fulfilment of certain formal requirements, its logic is symbolic; fiction has no necessary form, however, and it pretends to be speaking a literal language of realistic reportage, which is the antithesis of symbolism.

A novelist is liable therefore to have a hard time of it establishing the necessity of any misfortunes he chooses to let befall his characters. Indeed, he may not wish to establish any such thing: accident, bad luck, coincidence, and the like provide effects that would be the undoing of tragedy, but are natural to fiction, since they are, realistically speaking, more 'like life' (assuming, that is, that life for most people is more like the way it looks in novels than the way it looks in tragedy). A novelist may try to venture closer to tragedy by discovering some degree of blame for what happens in the characters themselves, either in the form of simple villainy, where misfortune is entirely the fault of someone else, or more subtly in the form of personal guilt, where individuals are seen to deserve, and thus in some sense to necessitate psychologically, the disaster they bring on themselves. However, even this kind of moral necessity, which often has to fall back on moralizing by means of rewards and punishments, where psychology alone fails to produce the desired result — that is, to explain why misfortune has to be

— falls generally far short of tragedy. The morality of tragedy is not one of blame, but of pity and fear; it is the kind of response we feel when we are convinced that men and events, wrong though they are, must be as they are — a response that is still moral, for it is concerned with what is good and bad in character and action, but a response touched by religious awe that such is the fateful frame of things.

It is worth reflecting on these differences and difficulties, which generally speaking prevent a novel from achieving the powerful effect of tragedy, in order to appreciate how much is being claimed for Tolstoy when we try to locate this tragic effect in *Anna Karenina*, and how rare an attainment it is, should it prove to be there. Does Tolstoy succeed in persuading us, then, that Anna's death is a tragedy, in the sense that no other outcome to her love for Vronsky is conceivable, and for reasons that transcend considerations of blame and disapproval? Certainly, few readers will interpret the moral theme of the novel, obvious though it may be, as expressing a morality of blame. Anna is too radiant and too likeable a figure for us to disapprove of her, and her behaviour is inspired by a quality of love too soul-possessing, too superior to worldly circumstance and considerations of self-interest for us to regret that she does not simply turn her back on it. The same rather fine impression is made by Vronsky, whose pursuit of Anna is represented with barely a hint of any selfish or ignoble motive, and who is ready to sacrifice his life, and does sacrifice his career, for the sake of his love. Some blame and much dislike do fall on Karenin, who is responsible for Anna finding heself in such a loveless home and so in need of emotional fulfilment. But Karenin is not made to play the role of villain; he is by no means the sole cause of the tragedy, and in his own way he is a victim. Society also is evidently blameworthy; its propensity for scandal, hypocrisy, and prejudice is intolerable — in fact, it shows up in a much worse light than Anna herself. By social standards, she is guilty of nothing more than a refusal to compromise and conform. At this rate, we might begin to wonder (with D. H. Lawrence) whether Anna does not deserve to prevail; for the spectacle of the better being crushed by the worse only strikes us as tragic if we can see why it has to be.

Why is a happier ending of Anna's story not conceivable? She is destroyed, Tolstoy makes it appear, not simply by reprehensible moral failings, in herself and in others, but also by some profounder necessity in the nature of things. Some sheer impossibility blocks her path; she can find no way to live in relation to her son, to her husband, or to her lover and their child. She lacks what was for Tolstoy the ideal and necessary centre of all human relationships, including the relationship of self through memory to its own past: she lacks a home. The imaginative significance of this lack for Tolstoy was so great that Anna is felt to be in jeopardy not only as regards her position in society, but in her life altogether. There is nothing for her to become, her love exists in a kind of vacuum, and cannot grow. Here the contrast with Levin and Kitty is particularly telling; their relationship can and does grow, they have in their family life more to occupy and sustain them than just their feelings for one another. Anna has only her love for Vronsky, and she is utterly vulnerable to every kind of doubt about his love for her; her happiness is always fragile and at risk, until the struggle against unhappiness becomes unendurable and overwhelms her. In the context of Tolstoy's moral realism, there is ultimately no place for the passion that consumes Anna. It resembles the passions of war, as they are represented in *War and Peace*: they too are emotionally irresistible, and the occasion of much exaltation and misery; and they too destroy themselves in the end, their heroism eclipsed by the familiar and enduring necessities of life. It is Tolstoy's imaginative mastery of these most recognizable conditions of common experience which enables him to convince us of the very real pressure forcing Anna to her destruction. The impression of tragic inevitability in *Anna Karenina* is an effect built up through the basic structure and cumulative weight of the novel's realism.

The composition of the real

What a huge and heartwarming pleasure it is to enter

Tolstoy's imaginative world! The place seems immediately lifelike, almost familiar, as though we could actually recognize it. In fact, the Russia Tolstoy knew, the scenery, the people, and their style of life, are quite remote, but they act and react and interact in ways we understand. This does not mean that we see here only eternal characteristics of human nature, unaffected by their historical and social situation. To be affected by one's place in society, which is in turn affected by history, is one of the most familiar features of human existence; the familiarity Tolstoy makes us feel certainly includes this feature too. The familiar feature, that is to say, is the felt effect of society and of history, rather than particular social and historical details, which may themselves well be unfamiliar. What we recognize to be realistic, therefore, is not any number of factual details, however exhaustive or accurate, but a combination of effects; and not all of these derive from external factors. Many are subjective, like the effect on us of passions or bodily conditions, or again of personality traits, habits, memories. Finally, there is the effect of action, the most familiar of all life's sensations, the feeling that we are in a position to do something — and are affected by things done to us. These are the effects which so-called mimetic literature simulates, by combining different elements and aspects of experience, between which some effective relationship becomes apparent. Only in relationship to other things, and especially to other kinds of thing, can the effectiveness of anything be felt; the effect of the real consists in the connections between things rather than in things themselves. Thus, the primary effect of narrative is to connect a story with its principal actors, so that we feel we recognize them because we know what happens to them and recognize the story because we know who enacts it. Neither they nor the circumstances of their particular story may be at all familiar to us in themselves, but the connection between them is. And the number of connections which the novel is able to establish, thanks to the freedom and openness of its form, is very large, going far beyond the simple effects of storytelling. The much increased scope of its material only adds to its realism where it serves to produce a more complex unity of connective relationships and effects, without which it is not lifelike but lifeless.

Tolstoy himself wrote in a letter of the importance of what he called 'the endless labyrinth of linkings in which the essence of art resides'. The task of criticism, he declared, was to guide readers through this labyrinth 'to those laws that serve as the basis of these linkings' (23 April 1876). However, he also warned that it is 'impossible to express the basis of this linking in words', and observed that 'if I wanted to say in words everything that I had it in mind to express in the novel, I should have to write the very novel that I have written all over again'. There is evidently for Tolstoy something substantially present in life, and now also in his successfully lifelike novel, which cannot be reduced to explanatory words, 'Each idea,' he went on, 'expressed in words on its own, loses its meaning, is terribly reduced, when it is taken alone out of the linking in which it is found.' As regards the linking itself, or what we have referred to as the connections between things, Tolstoy suggested that 'it is effected I think not by ideas but by something else . . . it can only be expressed indirectly, by words describing images, actions, situations'. Another letter gives a further clue to the subtlety of the links which Tolstoy believed gave unity to *Anna Karenina*: 'The structural links do not rest on the plot or on the relationships (the acquaintance) of the characters, but on internal linking' (27 Jan. 1878). This indicates that we need to do more than look at the broad thematic and moral connections in *Anna Karenina*; it is time now to examine more closely the basic composition of Tolstoy's realism, on which ultimately the tragic effect of the novel rests.

The opening chapter is a masterpiece of realistic art. Tolstoy fulfils one of the first conditions of liveliness in narrative − it is tempting to overlook the artistic illusion and say one of the first conditions of life − by at once having something happen. The reader is plunged into the turmoil of events within the Oblonsky household where 'everything had gone wrong. The wife had found out about her husband's relationship with their former French governess and had announced that she could not go on living in the same house with him.' There follows such a catalogue of domestic goings-on, servants leaving and children not looked after and husband not returning home, that we see something else is needed to turn events into action. A mass of events begins to look more like what Tolstoy calls them here: a situation, a state of affairs. The other component of action is the role of particular people in it, whose story it becomes; stories, like time itself, pass objectively in the world, but also subjectively in the life of this and that individual. Fiction is thus in a unique position to evoke the 'reality' of stories, thanks to the convention which allows it to see both sides of them at once, innermost feelings and thoughts as well as outward events, and to pass freely from one to the other, sometimes in the same sentence. Tolstoy chooses to make the story of these events the husband's rather than the wife's, and the moment when they acquire the semblance of actual experience is when Stiva Oblonsky wakes up on the third day of domestic crisis in his home and remembers what has happened.

The scene looks simple enough, but in the number of elements it combines and relationships it sets up it is a most subtle display of novelistic effects. As if to emphasize the composite character of reality, Tolstoy assembles two of the biggest components in slow motion, indicating the gap which doubtless always exists, though it is mostly overlooked, between external fact and internal experience. Oblonsky has been dreaming and his mind is still preoccupied with his dream; he has not yet realized where he is — in his study instead of in his wife's bedroom — nor remembered what has happened. The dream is everything Freud, some decades later, might have expected of a man who does not want to remember, who would prefer to be somewhere else, who wishes unconsciously and without neurotic complication for wine, women, and song. There is so much that is 'nice, very nice' in this utterly inner world, which never makes contact with reality, being below the level at which it can 'be expressed in words or even thought about clearly'. No wonder

Oblonsky hugs his pillow, 'as though wishing to sleep for a long time'. And then, after groping around in a half-conscious and still contented state between waking and dreaming, he wakes up completely, and has to face the reality of his situation. It is a reality which Tolstoy continues to represent subjectively: the events which follow take place now entirely within Oblonsky's mind. As he recalls them, they exist again purely as mental effects; nothing else 'really' happens here and now in the study where this scene is set.

We are so used to the technique of the flashback in narrative that we easily overlook the significance of what Tolstoy has decided to do here. He might have recounted this scene, in which Oblonsky is confronted with his wife's discovery of his infidelity, in the time and place when it actually occurred. By presenting it as it recurs, obviously not for the first time, in Oblonsky's tormented memory, Tolstoy is exploring a further possibility within the mode of writing already introduced by the dream: the mode which concerns itself with all that side of life which is inward and invisible. It is remarkable how much the addition of this intangible and unseen dimension to the objective surface of events contributes to their solidity and gravity and lifelikeness. The character of this scene, for instance, has in effect changed in the interval since it happened. Three days before, Oblonsky had come home in a characteristically light-hearted mood, 'with a huge pear in his hand for his wife' — the kind of easy gesture he always expects will smooth his way through the world — to find Dolly holding the wretched note that revealed everything. His only reply to her angry and desperate questions had been to 'smile his habitual, kind, and somewhat foolish smile'. It must have made a memorable enough scene at the time, but as a scene in Oblonsky's memory it has assumed a quite distinct significance. That smile has become the focus of his attention; he regards it almost as the explanation of why everything has gone wrong: '"It's all because of that silly smile", thought Oblonsky.' This is evidently what 'he could not forgive himself'; his mind is still preoccupied by wondering why he did it ('by a reflex action of the brain', he tries to tell himself), and by imagining what else he might have done: 'taking offence or denying the whole thing, justifying himself or begging forgiveness or even remaining indifferent – any of which would have been better than what he actually did'.

It is in the light of such reflections as these that the original unhappy scene is now re-presented. Tolstoy might have made such moral comments directly to the reader while describing the scene as it first occurred, but they would in that case have been much less effective, because they would not have appeared to be an integral part of Oblonsky's experience, which would have been left looking rather empty and fatuous as a result. By means of this flashback, Tolstoy adds to Stiva's rather mindless encounter with his wife the 'depth' of his nagging recollection of it.

Tolstoy adds, of course, something else besides, which is more than simply a realistic effect: namely, his own uniquely profound and moral insight into Oblonsky's moment of self-awareness. Criticism is caught in a dilemma: it cannot, on the one hand, speak as though Oblonsky's self-awareness were some kind of real original, which could be thought about separately from Tolstoy's own intelligent formulation of it. On the other hand, it also cannot treat these two things as quite identical, because Tolstoy's moral vision is clearly superior to Oblonsky's. This superiority is moral in the sense that has been mentioned already: it is based on Tolstoy's imaginative grasp, which he shares with the reader, of all the elements comprising the reality not only of this scene but of the entire novel – a morality which insists less on what is good and bad than on what is necessary and cannot be otherwise. Oblonsky obviously cannot see himself quite as we see him, for all that he is said to be 'a straightforward man in his dealings with himself'. We see that he is after all faithful to his home and his wife after his fashion; he is worried at the disruption, but clearly wishes for a resumption, of his family life; he wants things to go on as before. This tells us something – which we shall have plenty of occasions in this novel to remember – about the essential triviality of the love affairs he conducts, which are a pleasant amusement to him or at most the fulfilment of a physical, and he thinks therefore justifiable, need. After all, he is a handsome, susceptible man of thirty-four, whose wife 'was already faded and plain and no longer young, a simple uninteresting woman; so it seemed to him that she really ought to be indulgent. But it proved to be quite the opposite.' Tolstoy is here enjoying one of the effects which is realistic in a subtle stylistic and compositional sense, rather than in any literal one. He phrases his observations almost, but not quite, in the words Oblonsky might have used, and derives a humorous irony from the difference: the difference between Oblonsky's moral awareness and his own. The truth of the observation – its realism – exists in the play between the observer and the thing observed. We are in a position to recognize how much this man's character depends on his bodily constitution and physical temperament, and indeed on all the other circumstances which make up his situation in the world, but we know that Oblonsky is not in the same position and does not share this insight. He even comes close to voicing in this first chapter the moral conclusion of the novel to come; '"I am to blame and yet I am not to blame. That is the whole tragedy."' But he trivializes this insight, like everything else. His merely worldly wisdom in the face of life's inescapable realities resembles a complacent shrug, which is the opposite of Tolstoy's truly tragic vision.

We are, however, in these opening pages of the novel made more aware of Oblonsky's bodily presence than of his spiritual one. No writer understands better than Tolstoy the part played by the body in human experience, not only in the great activities of love and work and war, but in all the most common gestures of daily behaviour and communication. He does not exaggerate this part, as so-called naturalists and other modernists have subsequently done. His realism explores the moral effect the body may have in actual life, rather than the sensational fantasies it may give rise to in writing. In his descriptions he has no difficulty in observing the proprieties customary in his day, which censorship would have reinforced had it ever occurred to him to break them.

When Dolly's children are guilty of some misdemeanour behind the raspberry canes, causing their harassed mother yet more weariness with their 'nasty tendencies', we are not told what exactly they were up to. Nor is it necessary that we should be, as far as Tolstoy's moral realism is concerned, which gives us more important things to think about. It would certainly be wrong to suppose that moral in this context means merely keeping one's eyes shut to conventionally less mentionable parts or functions of the body; it means rather keeping them open to the body's psychic significance, its effect on personality and consciousness (including other people's), without which the facts alone are likely to have a merely prurient interest. Tolstoy's realism discovers more significance in the bodily constitution and situation of his characters than most of his contemporaries can show, even the notorious French naturalist writers; for if the body is for him too the foundation of human existence, it is the foundation of something much bigger than itself. The parts it plays are as various as the characters themselves.

Description of a character's physical appearance was a conventional form of introduction in the realist novel; in introducing Oblonsky, Tolstoy at once shows that he has a better use for this, as for so many other kinds of realistic detail. We first meet Stiva lying on a morocco-leather couch in his study, and the first thing we see him do is 'turn his plump, pampered body over on the springs and hug the pillow, pressing his cheek to it'. There might seem to be little room for moral observation here. Which man, when he is withdrawn into the inner recesses of sleep, is not wrapped there within himself, with a regard only − if Freud is right − for his own needs and satisfactions? Yet this image of Oblonsky as a self-regarding body expresses his temperament, his way of life, and his role in the novel, as a kind of *homme moyen sensuel*. He gets on well with everyone because he possesses in such generous measure, and is so spontaneously accommodating towards, that common physical nature in which all men share. He lives on good terms with them as he lives on good terms with himself, and his genial desire for

pleasantness and pleasure all round presents us with the
simplest form of relationship between a healthy body, easy
circumstances, and a not very highly developed intelligence.
Until something goes wrong, he can trust his body to know
its way around, as Tolstoy indicates by a detail when
Oblonsky begins to get up. Still half asleep, he cheerfully
looks for his slippers with his feet, slippers which his wife had
lovingly embroidered for him — and then, his equally unconscious movement of his hand to reach his dressing-gown
fails to find it in the place where it has hung in the bedroom
for the last nine years, and he at last remembers where he is
and what has happened.

In the chapters which follow, Oblonsky's robust good
health has its own way of resolving the moral crisis. 'The
answer is this: live from day to day, in other words, forget.
But as he could not find forgetfulness in sleep, at least not
until bed-time, nor return to the music [of his dream], he
must therefore lose himself in the dream of life,' The style of
these remarks does not sound much like Oblonsky; they echo
Schopenhauer's philosophy, and they belong with a rather
small group of reflections, which Tolstoy includes in the
novel on his own account, without embodying them in the
mind and personal manner of a particular character. The
reader must surely have understood well enough anyway what
Oblonsky's 'answer' is, as he slips into his confident routine
of living. His deep breath into powerful lungs, his vigorous
body and light step, his loud ring for the servants, their
immediate and friendly appearance, his conversation with his
valet as he sits before the mirror, in which they communicate
with one another perfectly: all this proclaims much better
than any philosophical theory the kind of balance which
exists in this man between his physical person and his
thoughts. A healthy balance, we might think, certainly a
popular one. The servants all like him; even the nurse, his
wife's 'best friend', is on his side. The general disturbance in
the house, as it was reported in the first paragraph, turns out
to be nothing like so acute in his presence. A kind of commonplace charm surrounds this man, whose natural capacity

for living is captured in the easy way he talks and gestures while being shaved. He personifies untroubled harmony of mind and body — in front of a mirror. What else is human life?

When Tolstoy writes in this physical vein, every detail he imagines communicates so much of life that further comment seems mere clumsy and unnecessary abstraction. Oblonsky's valet, for instance, enjoys looking after his master's person: 'Matvey blew some invisible speck off the shirt which he held ready gathered up like a horse's collar, and with evident satisfaction proceeded to envelop his master's carefully tended body.' We all know what that puff of breath at a non-existent speck of dust feels like, and in a sense what it means, though it is hard to put this into words: it suggests a moment of self-conscious pleasure in the whole activity of grooming Oblonsky, in sparing no effort, in doing the job perfectly, in feeling officious, self-important and slightly superior, as though indeed his master were a well-tended animal. Good grooming is an essential part of Oblonsky's life; we observe how he dresses, all the details of eau-de-Cologne, shirt cuffs, watch and chain, pocket-book, handkerchief, and so on, in a way that seems commonplace enough in a nineteenth-century novel, but which is not repeated for the other characters. This protracted account of Oblonsky's morning toilette may be a good way of establishing the realistic and domestic atmosphere of the novel generally — a getting-up scene to start the story off — and there is no character for whom such attentiveness to bodily concerns could have been more appropriate. And so to breakfast: 'In spite of his unhappiness, feeling clean, fragrant, physically well, and cheerful, he went, with a slight spring in each step, into the dining-room, where his coffee was already waiting for him.'

It is not long, then, before we realize the symbolic appro-priateness of that pear Oblonsky had been carrying, three days before; even the previous day, we are told, he had not forgotten to bring home sweets for the children — that is the sort of thing he remembers. For food is what he understands best — next to sex, which he understands in much the same way. He has a vague idea that he is being modern and

emancipated in his outlook: 'The whole aim of civilisation is
to make everything a source of enjoyment', he declares.
Through his portrait of Oblonsky Tolstoy is satirizing such
ideas, which he associates with the liberalism of the 1860s;
one particularly witty and telling simile characterizes Oblonsky's enjoyment of his liberal newspaper over his breakfast:
'Liberalism had become a habit with Oblonsky: he enjoyed
his newspaper, as he did his after-dinner cigar, for the slight
haze it produced in his brain.' Having finished the paper
along with his coffee and rolls, and shaking a crumb or two
from his waistcoat as he gets up, Oblonsky smiles happily:
'not because he felt particularly lighthearted – his happy
smile was simply the result of a good digestion'. True, this
happy smile 'instantly reminded him of everything, and he
became pensive', but Tolstoy's sentence reminds us of the
opposite fact, namely, that Oblonsky has been till then successfully distracted by breakfast and the news of the world
from his marital worries. Later this same day we find him at
table again, dining with Levin in a fashionable restaurant,
and happily absorbed once more in this most basic act of
living. Tolstoy describes at length the eager and thoughtful
concern Oblonsky shows over the menu in his desire to have
the very best dishes and wines; he feels at home here, the
waiters know and like him, his unpaid bills ensure that he
keeps coming back (a typically subtle observation of Tolstoy's
– this is consistently the same man who smiles at trouble, who
is physically incapable of feeling in the wrong, and makes a
virtue out of what cannot be helped). Levin provides a
wonderfully comic contrast; his conception of love is so high-
minded, so intensified by his solitary brooding in the country,
that he cannot imagine how he – obsessed as he is by feelings
of unworthiness and sin – could ever bring himself to declare
it. If he were not so desperate for reassurance, he would
not wish to speak of his love at all in such worldly surroundings, which seem to profane his feelings; when Oblonsky explains his own problem, Levin dismisses it as a quite different
matter merely of appetite and pleasure. But these are terms
Oblonsky quite frankly accepts, which is why he can never

find any other solution to his 'problem' than infidelity.

Oblonsky plays an important part in two further scenes, besides the one mentioned earlier (the dinner party he arranges with Levin, Kitty, Karenin, and others, which is central to the plot). In both of these we see him out shooting with Levin on Levin's estate, and both scenes concentrate so much on Levin's experience that they may count as his rather than Oblonsky's. However, Oblonsky affects Levin; he brings with him that change in the tone and feel and atmosphere of experience which is one major aspect of what we recognize as real in our relationship with others — a change almost in the person we feel ourselves to be. Levin does also go shooting by himself, but the occasions described here are associated with Oblonsky; and presumably he eats, but we never see him enjoy another meal like this one. In fact, it is Oblonsky who enjoys it, as he enjoys the shooting — and as he enjoys women. He has a great capacity for pleasure, for living in the moment, and for voicing his present satisfaction: 'Ah, this is life! How lovely! This is how I should like to live', he exclaims, as he seats himself comfortably in Levin's trap, after a good dinner, with a cigar in his mouth, and the prospect of a good shoot before him (II, 14). This is part of the reason why people like him: they know that with Stiva you enjoy yourself. Levin feels this as soon as he recognizes who his visitor is, and Tolstoy makes clear what kind of delight he experiences by contrasting with it the willed moral joy of receiving his difficult brother, whose visit Levin dreads. Oblonsky is the right man for Levin's 'happy mood of spring', just as he is the right man to talk to about love, quite apart from his family connection with Kitty. Levin may not be able to enter into his friend's enthusiasm for ever new amorous encounters, but he can be sure Oblonsky will understand his own. He at first lacks the courage to speak, but out shooting in the dusk Levin finally risks it. Tolstoy mentions that the two men were standing 'some fifteen paces apart', a detail which contributes strongly to the impression of realism, because it tells us something: namely, the kind of bond which this situation has established, the effect which being out shooting with Oblonsky has on Levin.

   Scenes of this kind have long been appreciated as amongst
Tolstoy's best, and it is important to explain why he is so
good at them — not just in autobiographical terms (he used
to go hunting and knew what it was like), but in artistic ones.
Tolstoy does more than report accurate details of such
experience: he understands its physical and spiritual effect.
Hunting, like all sport, and of course fighting in war, changes
our apprehension of reality, beginning with the pitch of feeling, the focus of attention, the awareness and control of the
body, and extending to vivid impressions of the physical
environment, and above all to the immediacy, suddenness
and succession of events. Experience becomes extraordinarily
confined to the moment, and the distance between thought
and being is tightly reduced, so that a unity of self-awareness
and awareness of the world is produced, which seems to make
the reality of such moments more intense — as though reality
admitted of degrees. Such experience comes naturally to
Oblonsky, who is a good sportsman. Levin, we discover in the
second hunting scene, is liable to have off days, as a result of
his highly introverted moral character: his determination to
suppress his natural feelings of dislike for another member of
the shoot quite spoils his aim. Success and failure in shooting,
hunting, or any kind of sport, spring from peculiarly profound causes, which involve the whole person and more
besides; and their effect is no less profound, because it seems
to indicate more than can be consciously understood or
accounted for. Beyond the reach of thought and conscious
deliberation, the body performs according to mysterious
aptitudes of its own, and beyond the reach of the person
altogether lies a realm of chance. A successful aim and
especially a run of luck give the exhilarating feel of something
immensely good — a harmony perhaps of mind and body and
circumstance, or some form of mastery or ascendancy. A
moralist might be inclined to find a negative word for it;
Tolstoy does not define it at all, but conveys its unmistakable
emotional effect of triumphant delight, as well as its contrary,
nervous and depressed exasperation. His most brilliant touch,
which strikes us oddly enough as a superlative bit of realism,

is to include the experience — the actual thoughts and feelings — of Levin's dog, Laska. This could so easily sound silly and sentimental, but it convinces us because she possesses to a much higher degree than Levin that intuitive and total relationship to her physical surroundings which hunting requires. The implication that the hunter's pleasure is closely akin to animal high spirits, and that human concerns and conversation are, from the point of view of hunting, an irrelevant distraction (as Laska thinks), does not disturb Tolstoy. In all his descriptions of physical encounter and crisis, Tolstoy evokes their further effect of enclosing a person within his own experience and, at least momentarily, isolating him from others. This does not necessarily destroy all personal bonds; on the contrary, there may be a deep sense of sharing, of common participation in life's nameless reality, between sportsmen or between soldiers — and, of course, between lovers.

In Tolstoy's composition of a realistic canvas, it is physical components like these which create some of the most striking and memorable effects. They are never — let it be stressed again — an end in themselves; indeed, they are effective precisely because of the way they are combined with other aspects of experience, with which they interact to produce a mutual modification. Tolstoy is especially skilful at noting, for instance, small gestures which accompany spoken words or inner thoughts and help to reveal their unvoiced significance. This significance is of a quite simple kind: to see it requires no great subtlety of interpretation, no search for a hidden meaning — indeed, the significance is substantial rather than cerebral. A hundred examples might be cited from *Anna Karenina*, but two or three must suffice. In the scene in which Vronsky boldly declares his love and Anna feebly protests, she listens to his last passionate words just as she is leaving. The coachman restrains with difficulty the restive horses; a footman waits with his hand on the carriage door; the hall porter holds the great door of the house. These three waiting figures exude an atmosphere of delayed and slow departure. (We have been told in passing earlier that Anna has stayed on to supper, refusing to return home with

Karenin; the horses are restive from long standing in the cold.) And Anna? 'Anna Arkadyevna was disentangling with her little deft hand the lace of her sleeve from a hook on her fur cloak, and with bent head she was listening with rapture to what Vronsky was saying, as he escorted her' (II, 7). There is no obtrusive symbolism in any of these details, neither the rearing horse nor the entangled lace; but there is great emotional eloquence in Anna's bent head and in the movements of her fascinating hand, which we watch as Vronsky does — surely pausing in the doorway in the process, though the text does not say so. And we feel the effect upon Vronsky as she repeats the word 'love' slowly to herself, and then glances up into his face, suddenly, as she gets the lace disentangled. The significance of what she says to him we shall have occasion to consider later; at this moment he scarcely takes it in himself, but responds utterly to her physical presence and gesture and glance.

Much later, when Anna's effect on Vronsky is evidently no less powerful but much more disturbing and destructive, another gesture — of his this time — embodies its altered character. They are living together and have returned to Petersburg, where she insists on appearing in public at the opera, dressed in a sensational Parisian gown. Vronsky is aghast, fearful of the consequences of provoking and flouting public opinion in this way; her beauty irritates him now, and he is angry at her behaviour — yet he cannot explain to her frankly the reason for his anger. Tolstoy contributes many other touches to render the complex emotional reality of the scene, in which their intense feeling for one another is twisted with misunderstanding and inner anguish. Vronsky remains for a while alone in his room, imagining Anna's arrival at the opera, taking off her cloak, stepping forwards into the light. Is he afraid? Is he leaving others to protect her? With a gesture of despair, as he paces about, he realizes what a stupid position he is in:

With this gesture he caught against a small table on which was standing a bottle of seltzer water and a decanter of brandy, and nearly knocked it over. He tried to steady it, lost hold of it, then kicked the table angrily and rang the bell.   (V, 33)

Tolstoy has done no more than describe a very understandable reflex movement, but he communicates through it a quite precise impression of Vronsky's psychological state. We need no elaborate theory of displaced or transferred emotion to understand here how dissatisfied Vronsky is with himself, and how distracted. This trivial accident and his reaction to it are an obvious indication of how upset he is; his physical clumsiness expresses the awkwardness of his situation; whatever he tries to do now to put things right only makes them worse. There is even a hint perhaps of something more besides, which is suggested by what Tolstoy has already shown us of states in which mind and body are perfectly in harmony, signifying happiness and goodness, and states in which they are not. This is a lesson which we have watched Levin learn earlier in the novel.

It is said of Levin that once, after losing his temper with his bailiff, he had recourse to a remedy of his own: he had taken a scythe from one of his peasants and had himself started to mow. Tolstoy describes another occasion on which Levin, irritated by the observations of an intellectual trying to put him in the wrong decides (since it is the season) to go mowing with the peasants on the following day. The experience occupies two chapters; even though these have nothing to do with either of the two love stories, his own or Anna's, they constitute a strong point in the moral framework of the book and a solid component of its realism. The climax of this experience is described in very similar words three times; we are given a very clear idea of Levin's spiritual state, which forms the culminating discovery of the first of the two chapters, and then in the second the increasingly sure knowledge which sustains Levin through the heat of the long day's work:

A change began to come over his work, which gave him immense satisfaction. In the middle of his work there came for him minutes during which he forgot what he was doing; it became easy for him, and in these same minutes his swath came out almost as even and good as Titus's. But as soon as he remembered what he was doing, and started to try to do it better, he immediately experienced the whole difficulty of the work, and his swath came out badly.(III, 4)

More and more often those minutes of unconsciousness came, when it was possible not to think about what one was doing. The scythe cut of itself. Those were happy minutes.

The more Levin mowed, the more and more often he felt minutes of oblivion, in which it was not his arms which swung the scythe, but the scythe moved of itself, a body full of life and conscious of itself, and as though by magic, without a thought about it, the work did itself correctly and distinctly. These were the most blessed minutes.

(III, 5)

What we read as an idea is not one for Levin, of course; for him this experience is at the furthest remove from conscious and deliberate thought. This is one reason why it is so important to him: he has turned to physical activity out of frustration with intellectual debate. The repetition of this 'idea' in the text expresses its real significance, which lies in the fact, so to speak, that it 'really' happens and keeps on happening. The text becomes a kind of record of the objective and physical conditions which tangibly make this most important spiritual experience possible. It belies any notion that spiritual significance must necessarily be something that is thought; and Tolstoy does not reflect upon it any further or offer any moral or psychological explanations. In telling us what this experience is like, he confines his style most remarkably and most effectively to the material circumstances of the event. He uses almost no similes or metaphors throughout the two chapters; those that do occur — 'as though by magic', 'a swath mown straight as a thread' — attract no imaginative attention to themselves but serve only to render some concrete particular more precise.

As is often the case, Tolstoy works with quite plain and precise phrases, which he has no hesitation in repeating. Translators tend to disguise or soften their effect by skilful use of synonyms and variants or by simple omission: it is not hard, for instance, to avoid the repetition of 'work' and 'minutes' in the first extract (the usually preferred English word 'moment' can also be repeated less noticeably than the Russian *minuta*). Other repetitions which are usually and easily avoided have been retained in the translation given

above, while a number of idiomatic, verbal usages have been
rendered as literally as possible — not because the resultant
clumsiness corresponds to Tolstoy's Russian, but in order to
give an impression at least of the almost pedantic concreteness and insistent particularity of his style. Once he has
chosen the defining word for a particular thing he goes on
using it, regardless of the number of times he may need to put
it down. For instance, the word translated above as 'swath'
is *ryad*, which means simply 'row', and Tolstoy uses it
twenty-eight times. The Russian language appears even to
conspire with his stylistic intentions, or say rather that he
knows how to exploit its resources for his own ends, for the
words connected with mowing — 'mow', 'cut', 'haymaking',
'scythe', besides one or two further forms of the word
(*kos'ba*, *prokos*) for which there is no English equivalent —
are all recognizably similar, since they derive from a common
root (*kosit'*). Tolstoy achieves his essential effect, however, as
a result less of choosing particular words than of thinking
always about the same concrete components of Levin's
experience. Such toil on the land represents for Tolstoy's
imagination a basic condition of human life, and there is
a hint of epic ritual in his repetitions. He thinks with great
particularity of general and universal experiences: of
endurance and difficulty, of movement, heat, fatigue and
work, with a group of men united and equal in a common
task. These are like the terms of a single great idea, each one
of which has to be learned concretely, by hard repeated use,
until it becomes familiar, self-evident, and takes its place in
the final, complete realization, which means nothing other
than that it has really been lived; it is understood fundamentally as life is understood, simply by being known, together
with all the things which help to make it what it is and which
are joined in the completeness of this experience — the sweat,
the water, the repose, the shade, the mushrooms in the grass
. . . Whatever truth it is that Levin learns through the long
course of this one day, it is identical with the toil and achievement of the day's work, not a thought in his mind, but a part
of his life.

Beauty

With Stiva Oblonsky, Tolstoy establishes the basic colours of
the body on his canvas of the real: its commonplace needs and
satisfactions and selfishness, its universality. With his sister,
Anna, he lends these same colours greater intensity and depth
in the attractiveness and longing of sexual beauty. Her beauty
has a lot in common with her brother's likeable appearance;
people smile when they see her, they instantly like her, women
and children as well as men. Anna and Stiva resemble one
another also in their vitality, which is what lends radiance to
their features, and causes them to walk with the same firm
step. She shares with him too a liveliness of manner, a
readiness of sympathy and emotional responsiveness to
others, and a capacity for living intensely in the moment. This
temperamental and physical likeness to Stiva contributes to
the effect her story has on us, at least in its early stages; for
we know already from the outset into what adventures his
temperament has led him. We have heard his frank views
about the way of the world and especially of the flesh; we cannot help being impressed by his amiability and may even be
persuaded that his behaviour really cannot be all that bad,
since he so obviously means no harm. We are not surprised,
in fact, that Anna should inspire and need love; what we are
not prepared for, any more than her brother, is the intensity
of her passion. She sounds so understanding and sensible in
dealing with her brother's misdemeanours, so well able to
restore good relations between him and Dolly, so confident
that there is nothing here to cause irreparable unhappiness. It
is one of the masterly ironies of the novel that Tolstoy first
shows her playing this role, which later Stiva and Dolly find
themselves quite unable to play for her. At some rather profound level we discover also in this carefully composed
artistic effect a darkly familiar feature of real life: that the
healer cannot heal herself.

In one further respect also, Anna resembles her brother:
like him, she does not feel that she is to blame. Remembering
how she had taken Vronsky away from Kitty, she says: 'But

I was not to blame. And who is to blame? What does being to blame mean? Could things have been otherwise?' (VI, 23). Her words echo Stiva's first reflections in the novel, in which he announces, albeit in a not yet entirely serious context, its tragic theme. By the time Anna speaks them, the tone of the novel has changed considerably. The moral question has been rendered more acute: how responsible are we for the way we are made and the way things are? In Stiva's case, the argument that 'it's no use denying facts . . . [when] your wife is getting old, and you are still full of life' sounds rather suspect, even frivolous, a mere plea for self-indulgence. But in Anna's case, the argument is rather harder to answer and much graver in its consequences. Is she responsible for her beauty of appearance and for the effect this has on other people? Can she help the situation she is in? Stiva tries to get her to see the matter in the sort of terms he understands:

'I'll begin from the beginning. You married a man twenty years older than yourself. You married him without love, or without knowing what love was. That was a mistake, let's admit it.'
'A fearful mistake!' said Anna.
'But I repeat — it's an accomplished fact. Then you had, let us say, the misfortune to fall in love with a man not your husband. that was a misfortune, but that too is an accomplished fact . . .' (IV, 21)

When Tolstoy adds the further bleak fact that Anna's marriage was the result of social scheming on the part of the aunt who brought her up, and who cared only about Karenin's position and prospects as governor of the province, he seems to want us to see Anna's plight in the same way her brother does. Indeed, when we consider all we know about Karenin's unloving and ambitious character, his apparent insensibility to Anna's beauty and his inability to respond to her emotional vitality, we find ourselves, even more than with Stiva, overwhelmingly on her side. No more persuasive case has ever been made in literature for the innocence of beauty, and it is one Tolstoy evidently wished to strengthen as he developed the portrait of Anna, by decreasing the elements of sexual coquettishness and sensual appeal in the earlier drafts, where she is the type *jolie laide*, and increasing her pure loveliness.

Yet for all that these are 'the facts', they have a significance very different from the entirely reasonable one which Oblonsky attributes to them. In the fate which befalls Anna, Tolstoy shows us much more than mistakes, and Oblonsky's belief in a solution is evidently futile. Her beauty and naturalness and love stand out radiantly against the prejudice and insensitivity which surround her; but between her beautiful nature and her situation in the world an interaction takes place for which indeed she is not to blame, but for which there is no help. She has a beauty of person which makes it unthinkable that she should seek any of the easy options her brother trades in.

Tolstoy makes us feel Anna's beauty by describing its effect upon others — and through them also on herself. When she enters the novel, stepping from the Petersburg train, she at once encounters Vronsky, who recognizes at a glance that she belongs to the highest society; and then he 'felt that he absolutely must look at her again — not only because she was very beautiful, or on account of the elegance and unassuming grace which were visible in her whole figure, but because in the expression of her lovely face, as she passed him, there was something tender and caressing' (I, 18). It is a wonderful entrance; like Vronksy, we know nothing about Anna, not even that this is Anna, and about Vronsky only that he is a brilliant young officer, who enjoys captivating women but has no intention of marrying one. We know enough, that is to say, to realize that a beautiful stranger on the Petersburg train is more in his line than young and inexperienced Kitty from a good family with definite ideas about marriage. And he is transfixed. Tolstoy does not actually say any such thing, of course; he simply describes what happens — or rather he renders his description of Anna as a kind of emotional happening. Her appearance seems to be an event, her very face seems to be alive with action: she too turns her head; her eyes rest on Vronsky, their thick lashes make them seem dark, but they are shining, and so attentive and friendly, that she seems to recognize him. Or does all that only seem so to him; is this an event in his mind? Just how much of it is lodged within and develops there as a realization of what he has just seen, Tolstoy makes clear in the following sentences. These sound like a simple continuation of the description of Anna, but in fact she has turned away; these are things which Vronsky must have noticed in that brief exchange of glances, and which are now present in his heart:

> . . . the suppressed animation which played over her face and flitted between her sparkling eyes and the slight smile curving her red lips. It was as though her nature were so brimming over with something that against her will it expressed itself now in a radiant look, now in a smile. She deliberately shrouded the light in her eyes, but in spite of herself it gleamed in the faintly perceptible smile.   (I, 18)

In these further lines, Anna's beauty continues to be felt as an effect of something that is happening − in her is it, or in her features, or in Vronsky's enthralled imagination? Doubtless, the only place where in the end anything can be said to occur is in the reader's mind: Tolstoy is introducing his heroine, and providing a description as custom requires. But what other novelist ever contrived so successfully to make the first description of his heroine coincide with the experience of love at first sight? We feel the reality of her beauty through the relationship it immediately establishes with Vronsky; we recognize its ancient sexual power to hold in thrall, to fascinate the lover's attention with every aspect of itself, and to inspire curiosity and a deep desire to know. We are exactly in Vronsky's position as we read on, eager to find out more about this woman: we listen with him to the sound of Anna's voice outside the carriage window, even though we do not understand the meaning of her conversation − one of Tolstoy's most extraordinary realistic touches is that he never does explain it (who is Ivan Petrovich?). We watch with him as Anna jumps down from the carriage 'with a light, sure step' and flings her arm around her brother's neck − 'a gesture that struck Vronsky by its decision and grace' − and kisses him. We feel what it is like not to be able to take our eyes off her and, with Vronsky, to smile 'without knowing why'; we feel in effect what Anna's beauty is like: it is *like this*. Vronsky immediately wants to count for something in this woman's life − and hears her say again that during the journey he has been the subject of conversation between herself and Vronsky's mother. In Anna's smile, in her manner, there is a hint of some special bond with him alone, over the head of Vronsky's mother who is seated while they stand; her parting smile and handshake confirm this feeling in him 'with joy'. The sight of her walking away talking eagerly with Oblonsky about something − 'something which obviously had no connection with him, Vronsky' − vexes him.

There follows the famous scene of the railway accident, in which a guard has been run over and killed. Readers with a lot of knowledge and literary experience, who know already how the novel will end, and remember the occurrence which inspired Tolstoy with this idea, and probably also remember the kind of literary precedents Tolstoy may well have had in mind (for instance, in Stendhal), tend to get fidgety at what they regard as too deliberate a novelistic effect. They positively squirm when Anna says: 'It is a bad omen.' They should not overlook, however, what can be said in appreciation of this nevertheless powerfully effective scene, the main point of which lies in Vronsky's behaviour and Anna's reaction to it − for without this her apprehension for the future must certainly appear rather far-fetched. When she speaks tearfully of a bad omen, she is also thinking about him, rather than just about the accident or its victim, as her next remark makes clear; he is now associated in her mind with that violent catastrophe, and indeed they both are − this fatal incident has brought them much closer together. What has happened is that Vronsky has used the opportunity to strengthen the unspoken bond between them; he has set himself with her apart from her brother and his mother. The opportunity presents itself with her agitated whisper of concern − not addressed to him − for the widow of the dead man, which contrasts at once with her brother's emotional chatter to Vronsky's mother. Stiva only thinks about his own feelings of horror, and within a few minutes he is chattering about something quite different. Vronsky appears perfectly composed until he hears Anna's whisper, to which he is immediately attentive; when he acts without saying anything, his silence does not suggest purely and simply the selflessness of modest virtue, but also a desire to carry out a wish of hers, to do something for her personally, rather than to perform a public good to which they all might have assented. It is this which is the bad omen; it is this which sticks in Anna's mind, though she does not like − but evidently cannot help − thinking about it. 'There had been something in the incident to do with her personally, that should not have been' (I, 20). Far from being a weak moment in the build-up of Tolstoy's realism, we have here a striking example of the effectiveness which external events owe to inward and unseen relationships; the effect of Anna's beauty is powerfully felt, like a new constituent part or a new dimension in the composition of a world rather commonplace by comparison − a world, one can imagine, in which it may not be assimilated but be destined to a disastrous future.

Anna's beauty does not affect Vronsky alone in this way, as Tolstoy reminds us again near the end of the novel, when Levin himself finally meets her. He stands spellbound before her portrait; like Vronsky long before, he cannot take his eyes off her. Suddenly he hears her conventional words of welcome to him, and on her lips these 'assumed a special significance for Levin's ears' (VII, 10). This sense of special significance dominates the interview for Levin, both the things she says − 'her smile and her look told him that she was addressing her words exclusively to him, esteeming his good opinion and at the same time sure in advance that they understood one another' − and even more the things he himself says and thinks: 'He, who had hitherto judged her so severely, now by some strange chain of reasoning thought only how to exonerate her.' The reader by this time is likely to be less dominated by the significance of Anna's beauty; he does not for one moment expect Levin to fall in love as Vronsky did, and it is no more than amusing to watch him lose his solemn head under her spell. From Levin's point of view the meeting is simply a rather small lesson in Tolstoy's favourite teaching on the subject of experience: namely, that things turn out to be very different from ideas we may have about them. Oblonsky tries to tell him this on their way together to Anna's: 'You'll see for yourself', he keeps saying in the face of Levin's rather chilly remarks and questions. In fact, even Oblonsky finds it hard (he gets very hot, Tolstoy notes, despite twelve degrees of frost) to keep up his characteristic tone of optimism when he thinks about his sister's present situation and her life of rather self-conscious 'interests' — in literature and art, in her daughter's upbringing, in caring for the children of a destitute English family, in writing a children's book. Stiva relies on his sister's charming presence to reassure himself and convince Levin that Anna really is a remarkable woman. And the charm works, of course; but the reader knows that this is no longer the point. This undeniably remarkable woman still has no difficulty in captivating a handful of men and convincing them that whatever they talk about with her is of wonderful importance; but we are not convinced, and neither is she. It sounds to us like affectation, as it does to Vronsky, who has seen it all before and grown tired of it; his absence from this scene explains much about it:

Though she had unconsciously been doing her utmost the whole evening to arouse in Levin a feeling of love — as she had lately fallen into the habit of doing with all the young men she met — yet . . . no sooner was he gone than she ceased to think of him. One thought, and one only, pursued her in different forms and refused to be shaken off. 'Why, if I have so much effect on others — on this married man who loves his wife — why is it *he* is so cold and indifferent?' (VII, 12)

Tolstoy also shows the effect of Anna's beauty upon women, and in particular on the two Shcherbatsky sisters, Kitty and Dolly. They both take to her at once, responding to her sympathetic warmth and friendliness; beyond that, they are each fascinated by her appearance in different ways, idealizing it, and even envying it. For Kitty there is mystery in it, a suggestion of 'another and higher world of complicated and poetic interests . . . "How I should like to know the whole romance of her life!" she thought.' She wants to see Anna at a ball, and imagines her wearing the kind of pretty dress she herself would wear; as soon as she does see Anna there, she realizes that her beauty has nothing to do with such prettiness. 'Her charm lay precisely in the fact that she always stood out from whatever she was wearing, that her dress was really not noticed.' Kitty is soon to be affected in a much more painful way by Anna's ravishing appearance:

She noticed that Anna was elated with success, a feeling Kitty herself knew so well. She saw that Anna was intoxicated with the admiration she had aroused. Knowing the feeling and the signs, she recognised them in Anna. She saw the quivering, flashing light in her eyes, the smile of happiness and excitement that involuntarily curved her lips, and the graceful sureness and ease of her movements . . . She seemed to be making an effort to restrain these signs of joy, but in spite of herself they appeared on her face.   (I, 23)

This is truly a masterstroke of Tolstoy's art, for in this scene he shows us much more than Kitty's shock of unhappiness as she sees that Vronsky is the cause of Anna's radiant look: he shows us in this most poignant way the whole character of the passion that, in this very moment, binds Vronsky and Anna. In its effect upon Kitty is concentrated all the reality of their nascent love, about which Tolstoy tells us little else besides, and which is felt in consequence to be quite fundamentally connected with their physical appearance and especially with Anna's beauty. Seen from the outside in this way, the external manifestation of love as a force acting upon two bodies makes a stronger impression than a meeting of two persons, just because their subjective reactions are not known. Some of the details of Anna's charm are familiar from her first encounter with Vronsky, when Tolstoy also said nothing about her feelings. He says nothing directly now, but by means of Kitty's feminine and jealous intuition we are made acutely aware of her exaltation and triumph. Similarly, all that Tolstoy himself never tells us about Vronsky's feelings is divined by Kitty as she gazes at the bewildered look of submission on his face − he had never looked at her like that!

What had become of his usually quiet, firm manner and tranquil, carefree expression? Now, every time he turned towards Anna, he bowed his head a little, as if wanting to fall at her feet in adoration, and his eyes held only submission and fear. 'I would not offend you', his every look seemed to say. 'I only want to save myself but I do not know how.' The expression on his face was one Kitty had never seen before . . . [it was] an expression like that of an intelligent dog conscious of having done wrong.

If Anna smiled, he smiled in reply. If she grew thoughtful, he looked serious. Some supernatural force drew Kitty's eyes to Anna's face. She was charming in her simple black gown, her rounded arms were charming with their bracelets, charming the firm neck with the string of pearls, charming the unruly curls, charming the graceful, easy movements of her little hands and feet, charming the lovely animated face: but in that charm there was something terrible and cruel. (I, 23)

Thus does Tolstoy depict, with quite memorable effect, the subject of great natural beauty and passion which — like sunsets for landscape artists — so easily shows up weaknesses in the realist's art. If the sophisticated reader starts to squirm again here, he has only to remind himself that this is how it all looks to Kitty. That anyway is the fiction created by the form of this passage, even if what it is made to contain by way of moral perception does occasionally exceed anything a young girl, even one in Kitty's circumstances, would probably think.

Kitty is witness to a scene for which she would naturally have the sharpest eye and keenest understanding; her sister is made witness to another one much later in the novel, after Anna and Vronsky have set up house together on his country estate, and for this Dolly, the faithful, long-suffering wife and mother, and instinctive, if weary home-maker, is the ideal observer. The visit provides a rare and welcome escape from her own home, and all sorts of usually suppressed thoughts come crowding into her head. Should she not have done the same as Anna, and left her husband? 'Passionate, impossible romances presented themselves to her fancy . . . with an imaginary composite figure, the ideal man who was in love with her' (VI, 16). How different it all is when she gets there, Tolstoy explains with his favourite moral lesson: 'As a general principle, in the abstract, Dolly approved of the step Anna had taken; but the sight of the man on whose account the step had been taken was disagreeable' (VI, 20). She is at first favourably impressed by Anna's appearance:

Dolly was struck by that fleeting beauty which comes to women when they are in love, and which she saw now on Anna's face. Everything about her: the pronounced dimples in her cheeks and chin, the curve of her lips, the smile that seemed to hover about her face, the light in her eyes, the grace and swiftness of her movements, her ringing voice . . . it was all peculiarly fascinating, and it seemed as if she herself were deliciously aware of it.   (VI, 17)

Tolstoy confirms this last impression later in the chapter, when Vronsky too notices 'her consciousness of her own beauty, and her desire that it should affect him'. There is never any doubt about Anna's beauty and her pleasure in the effect it has; it is shown off better than ever by the luxurious home Vronsky has provided and by her elegant clothes, which now evidently are rather more conspicuous, in Dolly's eyes anyway (for she knows what they cost). But the real issue for Dolly is a different one: is Anna happy in this new home, where she herself feels so uncomfortable? A visit to the nursery reveals how little Anna knows about her child by Vronsky or the child's two nurses; her remarks about how she intends to act on her doctor's advice to avoid having any more children shock Dolly; while Dolly's observation of the arrangements at dinner, conducted with the smooth formality of a dinner-party on the ever watchful orders of Vronsky, make her feel that Anna is a guest in her own home. Dolly becomes more and more convinced that Anna is not happy. She suddenly grasps the significance of Anna's strange new habit of half-closing her eyes. 'She remembered that it was just when her inner feelings were touched upon that Anna drooped her eyelids. "As if she half-shut her eyes to her own life, so as not to see everything", thought Dolly' (VI, 21). From her own homely experience, and an impulse too perhaps of feminine envy, she sees not only Anna's beauty but its fatal consequences:

Can Anna attract and hold Count Vronsky in that way? If that is all he looks for, he will find dresses and manners still more attractive and charming. And however white and shapely her bare arms, however beautiful her stately figure and her eager face under that black hair, he will find others still lovelier, just as my poor dear reprobate of a husband does.   (VI, 23)

Throughout this scene Tolstoy is passing judgement, of course, on Anna's moral deterioration; even Dolly's rediscovered liking for her own family by contrast — including 'dear reprobate' Stiva — quietly reinforces that judgement. It reaches us, however, not in the form of direct authorial disapproval, but through Dolly's sympathetic concern for Anna, and her acute and troubled eye for what makes a woman happy. Anna's beauty may still be undiminished; the mere thought of it still conjures up romantic possibilities. But Dolly learns, and so do we, that the 'promise of happiness' which love and beauty hold must be fulfilled in domesticity or suffer an inevitable defeat.

Love

'There are as many kinds of love as there are hearts', remarks Anna in the course of a typically frivolous conversation about love and marriage — early in the novel — in one of the fashionable drawing-rooms she frequents (II, 7). Vronsky is present, and the subject is spiced by everyone's awareness — and approval — of the relations between them; here Anna is generally liked and admired, while her husband is thought to be a fool. The setting is important, and it adds another dimension to the truth of her remark; hearts do not exist in a vacuum, nor do people, they are situated in circumstances which condition what they feel, think, and do. Had Anna been prompted to speak for her author, she might have added: 'and as many as there are situations'. Just what the situation is here in Petersburg, Tolstoy makes clear by means of a series of short chapters, full of minor characters and incidents, which contribute nothing to the plot but a great deal to the realism of Anna's and Vronsky's love story: to the impression, that is, that it is occurring in a real place, which impresses us precisely because it impinges on their love. Even the fact that they have fallen in love far away from here, in the perceptibly different social environment of Moscow, where Anna was merely visiting and Vronsky had only recently (and quite temporarily) settled, enhances this

impression; back here in Petersburg an air of unreality at first
hangs over their brief encounter. If their love is to be realized,
it will have to incorporate itself into the fabric of Petersburg
life; and what sort of life this is Tolstoy now also begins to
indicate by means of touches of contrast with Levin's quite
other life in the country. The day Vronsky comes back to his
old rooms to find two of his comrades gaily entertaining a
young baroness of very doubtful reputation, even he sees his
familiar surroundings for a moment with other eyes: 'Vronsky felt startled after the impression of a totally different
world he had brought back with him from Moscow; but at
once, as he might have put his feet into old slippers, he drop-
ped back into his former jolly, pleasant world' (I, 34). Here
everything is treated light-heartedly, including divorce, the
significance of events being judged by how good a joke they
become in the telling. When the coffee boils over, staining
clothes and carpet, it has done 'just what was required of it
– that is, it provided an excuse for noise and laughter'.

The effect upon the reader of these first scenes in
Petersburg, where Vronsky is seen in the daily round of his
own set, instead of appearing as a lone, romantic figure on
a railway platform and at a ball, is likely to be that we start
wondering what kind of love he will after all be capable of.
There seemed to be no doubt about this at his climactic
meeting with Anna in the middle of the night, at a brief train
stop between Moscow and Petersburg, when a snowstorm
obliterated all the world and destiny sided with passion to
bring them together. That was doubtless another scene to
make the sophisticated squirm (I, 30); its like has since
become the cliché of the cinema and television screen, where
a welter of such banal images are used to represent
tumultuous passion. Can anything better be said for Tolstoy's
version? This perhaps: that his realism is made of more solid
stuff than cheap metaphor. He is trying to depict a real interaction between circumstance and emotion; Vronsky and
Anna are drawn 'terribly close together' at this meeting, just
because they have no other relationship here to anyone or
anything – nothing else exists for them. Here the situation

is fully and completely defined for each of them by the presence of the other. There is, in effect, no situation apart from themselves, indeed no visible place here at all; the only reality is an emotional one, and this makes it seem almost natural that the wind should 'surmount all obstacles' at just this moment when their feelings do the same. Just as natural as that Anna should know why Vronsky is there before he tells her: 'To be where you are.' His words express the significance for both of them of his being there, rather than the purpose of his journey back to Petersburg. This meeting has been a moment of escape from that urbane reality and from its restraints, which Anna feebly tries to reassert. Their love will remain indelibly marked by these circumstances of its origin; its very lack of social relationship, so exultantly asserted in this unreal time and place, will one day be their undoing.

Just as it is a shock for Vronsky to see Anna with her husband, indeed to realize that she does have a husband, so it is for the reader a shock to see him, the great lover of the night before, back in 'his customary carefree Petersburg life'. Then he had felt that 'all his powers, hitherto dissipated and wasted, were now concentrated and bent with fearful energy on a single blissful goal' (I, 31). His ardour sounds less impressive when we hear of the attitude to such passions customary amongst his set: 'the important thing was to be elegant, handsome, broad-minded, daring, gay, and ready to surrender unblushingly to every passion and to laugh at everything else'. So confidently does he play the 'role of a man pursuing a married woman, who has made it the purpose of his life at all costs to draw her into adultery — a role that had something fine and grand about it' (II, 4), that it is hard to tell how far he is really in love. Tolstoy gives Vronsky at this point an entertaining escapade to narrate, which involves extricating two fellow officers from a bungled pursuit of a married woman, in order to show that Vronsky usually regards such matters in the light-hearted way society expects; the story, incidentally, was a true one (15? March 1874). Tolstoy achieves a further effect with this scene, however, which shows Vronsky acting as a kind of peace-maker, and helping to preserve social appearances; the part he plays recalls − though in an obviously less serious way − the one Anna played in patching up the Oblonskys' marriage. Some sort of contrast is evidently being suggested between the kinds of emotional problem Anna and Vronsky are familiar with in other people's lives and the emotional immediacy of their own; both of them are soon to discover that their own love affair is of an intensity and seriousness quite different from anything they are prepared for or know how to deal with. Tolstoy develops in various ways this kind of contrast, between the socially conventional view of love and its subjective reality. Anna becomes entangled in it during her first conversation with Vronsky after their nocturnal meeting on the train. She tries to forbid him to speak to her of love, to reprimand him for his bad behaviour towards Kitty, to appeal to his honour, even to make him believe that what she wishes is that he should go to Moscow and beg Kitty's forgiveness, and that they themselves should be just good friends. It is all palpably false; she has long been aware of her pleasure in seeing him, which is the reason why she frequents this particular section of society. Her very words of protest become a confession. No writer succeeds better than Tolstoy in making us feel the emotional effect of words, often − as here − by contrast with their intended meaning.

From the beginning, Tolstoy differentiates between Anna's feelings and Vronsky's, and this is important because in the end it is a difference which will tragically divide them. As Anna dozes in the train on her journey back to Petersburg, she feels that her nerves are being stretched more and more tightly; she is frightened of giving way to a nightmare state towards which she feels drawn: 'far from seeming dreadful, it was rather pleasant'. Tolstoy is making not a sloppy but a precise moral observation when he tells us, 'All the awfulness of the storm appeared to her now more beautiful than ever.' Such is the effect on her of seeing Vronsky here, and from now on her nervous tension becomes positively joyful and exhilarating, like the visions which fill her imagination. And yet she is being torn apart, to the point where she wonders, 'Am I myself or someone else?' It is a question that will recur; her love for Vronsky begins at once to threaten her identity. His love for her, on the other hand, intensifies and concentrates his character. His air of imperturbable composure now seems haughtier and more self-sufficient than before. His goal is clear and this makes him happy; he is proud − of her − but Tolstoy brilliantly observes how for him this is identical with being proud of himself. At their later meeting in society, Anna finds herself blushing and confused, resentful at being made to feel as if she 'were guilty of something'. There is quite simply no conflict in Vronsky's mind or situation; he boldly declares his love whenever he can. He knows the role is a fine one in society's eyes, and he plays it with dash, reciting lines which are so stereotyped that they sound quite artificial: 'I ask only one thing: I ask for the right to hope, to suffer as I do now. But if even that cannot be, command me to disappear, and I disappear. You shall not see me if my presence is distasteful to you' (II, 7). The very tone in which each of them speaks reveals how differently each understands the experience of love that they are courting; and inevitably so, for though they inhabit the same society they do not find themselves in the same situation within it. There is much truth in Anna's last remarks to Vronsky on this occasion:

'Love', she repeated slowly to herself, and suddenly, as she disentangled her lace, she added: 'I dislike the word because it means too much to me, far more than you can understand', and she glanced into his face. '*Au revoir!*' (II, 7)

These are the last words we hear Anna speak to Vronsky for 'almost a year'; we are shown nothing of their relationship during this time, and when − only a few pages later − we see them together again, Anna has surrendered herself to Vronsky completely. Three short intervening chapters deal with Karenin and Anna's relations with him: a rather surprising allocation of space and interest at this crucial juncture in the love story. Some allowance must be made doubtless for the discretion regarding sexual behaviour that was normal in the fiction of time; yet the absence of any indication of moral

doubt or struggle in Anna during this period is still surprising
— the more so in view of the attention Tolstoy pays later to
Anna's moral development, dilemma, and downfall. From an
artistic point of view, however, the effect of this foreshorten-
ing is rather powerful; it contributes to the impression of
fatality, and distracts from any question of blame. This effect
is reinforced by the character of Karenin, whose own inadequacies are more prominent at this stage than Anna's. As she
lies in bed beside him, her wide-open eyes bright with
thoughts of Vronsky, the fault still seems to be with Karenin,
who has dismally mishandled the only attempt he ever makes
to hold onto his wife; after attempting a few ineffectual moral
speeches, he goes off to sleep and snores, having found
nothing more to say to her. Anna's surrender to Vronsky is
explained implicitly by the loveless circumstances of her marriage, and for these Karenin appears to be entirely
responsible.

Anna's emotional nature is quite stifled in her marriage to
Karenin. Tolstoy's evocation of her profound and physical
antipathy to her husband provides some of the most
memorable details in the novel: Karenin's ears and walk and
habit of cracking his finger joints grate on the nerves. Nor is
his physical unattractiveness a merely gratuitous effect; it
embodies a kind of spiritual negativity and refusal. Karenin
does not want to acknowledge the reality of personal life, as
a living body of desires and ideas, especially not in his wife,
and scarcely even in himself. He is the man of routine, who
lives for his career in the ministry; he keeps up appearances
in order to hide behind them, and he has consequently very
little understanding of people or (Tolstoy remarks in passing)
of art. He embodies, to an extent that borders on caricature,
a social and bureaucratic code, by which he expects all
behaviour, thought and feeling to be rigidly regulated in
himself and in others. He thus becomes a foil for what
appears by contrast to be the natural and spontaneous passion of Anna, whose greatest desire is to tear down his
hypocritical and complacent front. Out of this contrast
between the artificial and the real, Tolstoy creates an implicit

moral valuation. Karenin is so unfeeling that he does not immediately notice Anna's relationship to Vronsky; he notices that other people notice it, and this worries him. He decides he must speak to her, not because he is jealous, but because 'there are certain laws of propriety which one cannot disregard with impunity'. When she pretends not to understand what he is talking about, he is prompted finally to say, with unwonted feeling: 'I am your husband, and I love you.' Her reaction is described as follows:

For an instant her face fell and the mocking light in her eyes died away; but the word 'love' roused her into revolt again. 'Love?' she thought. 'Can *he* love? If he hadn't heard there was such a thing as love he would never have used the word. He does not know what love is'.   (II, 9)

Do we believe her? During the course of this scene, Tolstoy achieves one of those effects which prevent his moral valuation from looking crudely black and white: it is Anna now who appears to be shutting reality out by putting up a front of pretence, indeed lies — her manner of light-hearted incomprehension is deliberately intended to make it impossible for Karenin to get through to her. He, on the other hand, is forced to see what he usually shuts out. With the help of a rather obvious metaphor — Tolstoy's metaphors are liable to sound clumsy in his predominantly non-figurative, concretely realistic style — Tolstoy explains:

Karenin was face to face with life — with the possibility of his wife's loving someone else — and this seemed to him very irrational and incomprehensible because it was life itself. All his life he had lived and worked in official spheres, having to do with mere reflections of life. And every time he had come up against life itself, he had stepped aside. Now he experienced a sensation such as a man might feel who, quietly crossing a bridge over a chasm, suddenly discovers that the bridge is broken and the abyss yawns below. The abyss was real life; the bridge that artificial existence Karenin had been leading.   (II, 8)

It would doubtless be going too far to suggest that the moral positions of Karenin and Anna are reversed, but it is none the less striking that, in the scene following her

seduction by Vronsky, Tolstoy describes Anna as closing her
conscious mind to a reality too painfully complex for her to
contemplate:

She not only found no words to express the complexity of her feelings, but she could not even find thoughts with which to reflect on
all that was in her soul.

She said to herself: 'No, I can't think about it now; by and by,
when I am calmer.' But that calm for reflection never came. Every
time she thought of what she had done and of what would become
of her and of what she ought to do, horror descended on her and
she drove these thoughts away. 'By and by,' she would say to
herself. 'By and by, when I am calmer.'

But in dreams, when she had no control over her thoughts, her
position appeared to her in all its ugly nakedness.   (II, 11)

Some readers nowadays may regard as suspect Tolstoy's
depiction of Anna's emotions *post coitum*: 'She felt so sinful,
so guilty . . . she had a physical sense of her degradation . . .
shame at her spiritual nakedness crushed her and infected
him.' Even more extreme are Vronsky's emotions: 'He felt
what a murderer must feel when he looks at the body he has
robbed of life . . . And, as with fury and passion the murderer
throws himself upon the body and drags it and hacks at it, so
he covered her face and shoulders with kisses.' It is certainly
not one of Tolstoy's happiest passages of style; as usual, the
figure of speech lets him down, being visually unsubtle and
unimaginative in a way his descriptions of actual things never
are. His view of the body here seems blurred, being half a
physical reality and half an idea; he both says that 'the body
he had robbed of life was their love, the first stage of their
love', while allowing Vronsky to cover it with kisses. Has
something unsettled Tolstoy's judgement at this point — for
instance, his own ambivalent feelings towards sex, which was
a powerful motive in his life, but also liable to arouse his
disgust? Vronsky might well be shaken to see what his 'one
absorbing desire' to conquer Anna has led to in her case, but
we have seen nothing in his character to suggest that he would
feel quite this violent revulsion: 'There was something
frightful and revolting in the recollection of what had been
paid for by this terrible price of shame.' It is tempting to

guess at possible reasons for the style of this passage — psychological reasons could perhaps be adduced, or moral ones, based on Tolstoy's biography, or more general historical reasons reflecting the difference between then and now — but such speculation would distract attention to matters extraneous to the novel, where (like it or not) the passage represents quite unforgettably a decisive crisis in the love story. And not primarily a crisis of sexual feelings either. Whatever the emotions aroused at first by their sexual relations — Tolstoy calls them 'shame, rapture, and horror' — these relations themselves are not in themselves the problem, but merely its occasion; perhaps this too is a mark of Tolstoy's realism, to recognize that lovers soon get used to physical intimacy. What has taken place, as a result of this intimacy, is a great and lasting change in their situation, and this continues to have a profound psychological effect. It is again Anna who senses what it is, when she exclaims: 'Everything is over, I have nothing but you left' (II, 11).

Tolstoy wrote of this scene: 'This is one of the passages on which the whole novel stands. If it is false, everything is false' (14? Feb. 1875). The love story of Anna and Vronsky enters now a new phase, which continues until they leave Russia in order to live together abroad. This phase is dominated by the pressure of the situation in which they find themselves, and by their ever stronger feeling that, one way or another, it must be resolved. Moreover, not only Anna is sensitive to this pressure; the situation does not bear on her alone. The real indication of how far the situation has changed is that Vronsky too is now aware of it; Anna after all had felt it before. In what does the change consist? Tolstoy depicts a complex interaction of social factors with psychological ones; he makes it impossible to disregard the influence of society on the lovers' feelings, but equally impossible to regard society as the sole cause of their distress. He is thus preparing the ground already here (in Parts II and III) for the inescapable tragedy later, which will be generated through fatal interactions between themselves and their situation. Undoubtedly, there is a shift in public opinion, which gets ready to vilify

Anna; Vronksy's mother, who had been notorious in her day, finds her son's liaison too desperate and Werther-like for her taste; there is talk of disapproval in high places, and this upsets Vronsky's brother. Vronsky allows no one to speak to him about his love, yet he is no longer invulnerable; he is sensitive to the merest hint of interference, which rouses him to 'a feeling of anger and hate — a feeling he rarely experienced . . . just because in his heart he felt that they were all of them right' (II, 21). Lying and deceit are foreign to his nature, but now on many occasions he cannot avoid them:

He felt all the torment of his own and her position, all the difficulty there was for him, conspicuous as they were to the eyes of the world, in concealing their love, in lying and deceiving; and having to lie, deceive, scheme, and constantly think about others when the passion which united them was so intense that they were both oblivious of everything but their love . . .

And for the first time the idea presented itself clearly that it was essential to put an end to this false position, and the sooner the better.   (II, 21)

The situation which Vronsky now clearly sees must be resolved is not only a social one but, in Anna's case, deeply domestic; for her the situation is much more complicated: she is a wife and above all a mother, and she cannot easily think of 'putting an end to this false position' with the same straightforward decisiveness that characterizes Vronsky. In this new phase of their love we learn more again about the subtle differences in their feelings, which are due to their respective positions as man and woman within their shared situation; each of them has a distinct social role and a distinct temperament, and again these are inextricably intertwined. Tolstoy immediately reminds Vronsky of the reason why he cannot simply throw up everything and go away with Anna: there is Seriozha, Anna's son. The boy's innocence causes them to act innocently in his presence; and the necessity for such acting arouses in Vronsky's essentially truthful nature the revulsion which he now often feels: 'against something: against Karenin, or himself, or the whole world — he hardly knew which', (It is a pity that Tolstoy decided to explain the moral significance of this emotion in Vronsky by means of one of his clumsy metaphors: the boy is the compass which shows them the error of their ways, II, 22.) Vronsky feels this revulsion for someone 'with tenfold force' when Anna tells him that she is expecting their child, and happily this time Tolstoy does not explain it; much later in the book the reader will see, if he does not guess it here, that as things stand a child of Vronsky's will still legally be a Karenin. There follows a scene in which their different reactions to the situation, resulting from their difference of position, gives a first hint of a rift between them. Anna still cannot think about her situation:

When she thought of her son, and his future attitude towards his mother, who had cast off his father, she was too terrified at what she had done to reason but, woman-like, only tried to reassure herself with false arguments and words in order that everything should remain as before and that she might forget the dreadful question of what would happen with her son.   (II, 23)

'Woman-like' has the ring of a prejudiced comment, but in fact what Tolstoy is observing, with his realistic sense of situation, is this: Anna behaves as she does because her position is essentially that of a woman, and this leaves her with no simple rational choice such as Vronsky wants to propose to her. Their conversation is a vivid example of a kind of exchange at which Tolstoy's genius excels: one in which we sense the pressure of unspoken considerations, of evasions and pretences, of things said unexpectedly and without clear purpose and reflection. Conversations are often like this in life, because we do not know where they will go, nor what is in the mind of others, perhaps not fully what is in our own; words trigger changes in meaning and mood in unforeseen ways. Conversations in literature generally tend to betray the fact that the author knows everything about them. Tolstoy understands better the real effect of conversation under the stress of great emotion; nothing sounds more lifelike than Vronsky's efforts to follow the twists and turns of Anna's speech.

Tolstoy's masterstroke at this juncture of the story is the introduction of the scenes at the race meeting, where Vronsky falls, and Anna betrays her love in public. These chapters exhibit great narrative skill; by recounting the event first from Vronsky's viewpoint, and then — after reaching the climactic fall — from Karenin's and Anna's, Tolstoy brings together the two different worlds in which his protagonists move, and makes us aware of the distance which separates them. Anna appears in both sequences of chapters; she leads now a double life, and the impossibility of her situation is cruelly and dramatically rendered in the moment of Vronsky's accident, when she can no longer contain her emotion before Karenin. Almost more drastic is the crisis in Vronsky's emotions; even though these have nothing to do with Anna, yet 'For the first time in his life he knew the bitterest kind of misfortune — misfortune beyond remedy, caused by his own fault' (II, 25). The placing of this incident in the story, the narrative elaboration of it to include scenes between the lovers and scenes between husband and wife, as well as Tolstoy's direct comparison of Vronsky's 'two passions' (for Anna and for horses), have the effect of turning the fatal accident which kills Vronsky's favourite mare into a kind of omen. After the crucial scene in which Anna and Vronsky have just made love, this event is the next thing to be narrated — as regards their love-story, at least; an interval of time is marked by chapters dealing with Levin. What Tolstoy failed to communicate very convincingly through his crude image of a murder, he powerfully suggests through his description of the jump, when Vronsky's careless movement in the saddle breaks the horse's back. This is not a symbolic suggestion, there is no hint of metaphor, even the word omen (which Tolstoy does not use) may imply too contrived an effect. Tolstoy is suggesting something altogether real, and no further praise is needed here of his ability to evoke the physical reality of such experience. Vronsky has killed the thing he loves; he is in despair; Anna in reckless desperation tells Karenin she hates him and loves Vronsky. As she and Vronsky prepare to meet that night, it is in the shadow of a disaster. The event is not symbolic, it is as purely and catastrophically real as a lost battle in a tragedy which decides the destiny of kings; it touches with ominous fatality the development of Anna's and Vronsky's love which comes now with her pregnancy.

The remaining scenes between Anna and Vronsky before they leave Russia together — that is to say, the meetings Tolstoy describes rather than merely alludes to — are clouded by misunderstanding. The lovers have less control over their passion, which in one sense grows stronger, but in another grows more dangerous and demonic, turning them into the puppets of their situation. The crisis and Anna's avowal to Karenin of her love for Vronsky do not produce that clarification of the situation or resolution of its tensions for which both long. Anna finds herself so crushed by the shamefulness of her position in her own home, which strikes her now as being 'absolutely hopeless', that she does not at once tell Vronsky what has happened. Her despair is partly due to the unfeeling determination of Karenin to preserve his own social position at all costs; Tolstoy paints a brilliantly damning picture of Karenin's priorities and motives, which encourages us to despise and even blame him as we never do Anna, for all that he is the innocent party. The effect of this will be discussed further in connection with Anna's tragedy; here we should notice how her situation debases her feelings even in her own eyes:

She wept because her dream of having her position cleared up and made definite had been destroyed for ever. She knew beforehand that everything would go on as it was — would, in fact, be far worse than before. She felt that the position she enjoyed in society, which had seemed of so little consequence that morning, was precious to her after all, and that she would not have the strength to exchange it for the shameful one of a woman who has deserted her husband and child to join her lover; that, however much she might struggle, she could not be stronger than herself. She would never know freedom in love, but would always be the guilty wife continually threatened with exposure, deceiving her husband for the sake of a disgraceful liaison with a man living apart and away from her, whose life she could never share.   (III, 16)

In time, Anna will exchange one shameful position for the other; but the fact that she is unable to imagine any positive outcome conveys already an impression of tragic fatality in her situation. All she can imagine, and soon begins to speak darkly about, is her death.

Their love continues, then, in a situation without any conceivable future; yet, even though it brings them now much less happiness and no hope, their passion becomes more important to them than ever. It is all they have. Each of them tries to resist disaster, to make a plan, to assert his or her will — and they both fail. Anna clutches at her son; Tolstoy remarks that she 'remembered the partly sincere, though greatly exaggerated role of the mother living for her son, which she had assumed during the last few years' (III, 15). Anna needs him now, because she needs an aim: 'the idea of decided action, binding her to her son, of going away somewhere with him immediately, made her feel calmer'. She packs, she writes a decisive letter to Karenin, but before she can send it she receives one from him, which re-establishes the situation Anna thought she had broken — and does so with menacing references to morality and the law (and with an envelope full of money). Vronksy makes an even more determined effort to think out his position, and Tolstoy undermines it by the simple device of allowing him to remain in ignorance of the fact that the situation has changed. The enumeration of Vronsky's code of principles at this point must result in comparison with Karenin's; for all their differences, they seem equally defective in the face of the crisis they confront. Vronsky believes he has it all sorted out: 'having made up his mind that he was happy in his love, that he sacrificed his ambition to it — or having, at any rate, assumed this role' (III, 21). He drives out to see Anna in a joyful mood of confidence that everything is beautiful, and within minutes he is for the first time in his life on the edge of tears. Never has a conversation between them gone so badly; the scene is a moving display of Tolstoy's insight into all that lies behind and beneath words. Vronsky can say nothing right, and least of all what he has been thinking, while she misinterprets even the expression on his face. Tolstoy never makes fully clear just what Vronsky did think; only later does he tell us that Vronsky had thought 'that it was better not to tie himself down' (III, 22), and later still again that he had even thought 'that they might part' (IV, 2). By now such thoughts are mere daydreams, and we wonder whether they could ever have been much more. 'He had stepped outside that circle of activity in which everything was definite, he had completely abandoned himself to his passion, and that passion was binding him more and more closely to her' (IV, 2).

It is a situation which cannot continue. They all, including Karenin, believe it must pass: 'Not one of them could have endured it for a single day, had it not been for the expectation of change' (IV, 1). But what change can there be? One way in which passion compensates for being thwarted is by imagining its own death, as Anna does. They will all be sorry, they will love her, they will remember her. And indeed, when she does fall ill after giving birth to her lover's child in her husband's home — a situation so spiritually painful as to be physically unendurable — Anna is magnificent. The near deaths of both Anna and Vronsky at this stage in the novel produce a most dramatic effect, but it is a quite temporary one. Their love story only seems to be coming to its inevitable and tragic end: there is a big but not final scene of moral reconciliation and farewell; there is a desperate but not fatal gesture by Vronsky who has lost too much to go on living. Just when he had discovered her, had come to love her as she should be loved, he had been humiliated before her and lost her for ever . . . and so on. And then it all turns out to be not like that at all. Life's typical chanciness decides that Anna shall not die but get better, and that Vronsky shall wound but not kill himself; with her return to health, Anna finds that moral admiration for her husband grows faint as feelings of physical repugnance for him revive, while Karenin himself feels his lofty sentiments of love and forgiveness are opposed by some 'brutal force' in the common course of life. Tolstoy's realism gains access to a whole new world by pursuing his lovers' story beyond its apparent culmination in a fine romantic death scene; the love story is over, and there begins what is in effect another story — of married life. A more grimly

inescapable tragedy awaits it there, which leaves no room for
fine spiritual gestures.

Married life

With the beginning of Anna's and Vronsky's life together,
and the marriage of Kitty and Levin, Tolstoy increasingly
exploits moral contrast as one of the central effects of the
novel; in the first half of the book it is present in a rather
more subdued and distant form. Tolstoy makes sure we
notice it now, by having the great event which transforms his
lovers into husbands and wives − for Kitty and Levin, their
marriage, for Anna and Vronsky, the decision to live together
− occur for the two couples at about the same time, and in
consecutive chapters. The contrast has the effect of throwing
into relief the distinctive moral character of each relationship,
which requires no further judgement from Tolstoy; these
utterly different experiences of love and marriage appear to
carry an inexorable moral law within themselves, whose
operation in one case indirectly explains what happens in
the other. The desperate suddenness with which Anna and
Vronsky find themselves again in one another's arms is
measured against the slow, shy, elaborate ritual of Levin's
engagement and wedding, his daze of happiness against
Anna's abandoned passion. 'There is something terrible in
this after all that has happened', she exclaims (IV, 22). She
and Vronsky are moved by a passion which in an instant
reduces to nought every other consideration and resolution;
it rejoices that nothing else matters. Unlike Levin and Kitty,
they have no plan for the future, no home to go to, indeed
no place in society where they can expect their new relationship to be accepted; content to live entirely for themselves,
they go abroad − while Kitty by contrast, intuitively
understanding her husband's deepest feelings and what
matters to him most, refuses a honeymoon abroad and insists
on settling at once in her new home in the country.
   Most striking of all in this context is the misunderstanding,
or total indifference to understanding, which marks the

reunion of Anna and Vronsky; this has its parallel too in the confusion of Kitty and Levin during their wedding, and is one of the most telling of Tolstoy's realistic effects, for it gives the exact feel of love's power to daze. But even here Tolstoy's moral discrimination is maintained. Anna and Vronsky behave as though nothing now stood in their way, but Anna herself puts back the very obstacle which Vronsky believes has been removed. When they leave Russia together, not only has she not obtained a divorce from Karenin, she has 'resolutely refused one'. In fact, she tells Vronsky at once that she does not want a divorce, explaining merely that she cannot accept Karenin's generosity; Vronsky cannot conceive how she can be thinking about such things in a moment like this: 'What did it all matter?' He forgets that he has come to her only because he has been told that Karenin does agree to a divorce; the news reached him at third hand — via Oblonsky and Betsy — and he never seeks or gets confirmation of it from Anna. But before hearing that mere unconfirmed rumour, Vronsky was making ready to bury himself in official duties in remote Tashkent, and Anna was meditating fine speeches, doubtless of farewell. He does not give another thought either to the question of divorce or to his post in Tashkent, which he resigns, thus putting an end to his career. His disregard of the world at this moment is truly heroic, and Anna is swept away by it — but not blinded. She still thinks: 'O why did I not die? It would have been better', and weeps bitterly. Does she sense that precisely these worldly realities, the question of divorce and of Vronsky's future occupation, will return to plague them? As their life together begins, they have certainly lost the world, but not well.

Levin's love story has from the start been dominated by his desire to marry:

He could not imagine love for a woman outside marriage, and he even pictured a family first and then the woman who would give him the family. His ideas about marriage therefore did not resemble those of the majority of his acquaintances, for whom getting married was only one of the numerous facts of social life. For Levin it was the principal thing in life, on which its whole happiness turned.

(I, 27)

Levin has apparently never approached Kitty with any thought in his head other than whether she will agree to become his wife, and as a result he feels overwhelmed at so tremendous a prospect whenever he sees or thinks of her. The physical immediacy of the scenes in which Anna and Vronsky fall in love − and even more obviously of Stiva's love affairs, which Levin simply cannot understand − is counterbalanced in his case by a kind of imaginative awe, which Tolstoy half humorously shows to be out of all proportion to the rather ordinary little girl Kitty is, while half making us feel also, on another plane of awareness altogether, that this awe is totally appropriate to the real wonder of a human being and of human love. Levin's feelings seem often to be sublimely unworldly, so much so that they make him socially gauche, but they are also quite down to earth; he imagines his wife-to-be not only as the sum of all perfection but also as fitting into his everyday life: 'I and my wife will go out with our guests to see the herd come in . . .' As Oblonsky tells him: 'You're very much all of a piece . . . you want love and family life to be indivisible' (I, 11). Tolstoy endows Levin with much of his own piety towards family life, which was, as we have already noticed, intimately linked with memories of his childhood; thus in the enchanted world into which Kitty's smile transports him, Levin feels the way he remembers feeling on rare occasions in early childhood − full of a tender, calm, sweet emotion. Tolstoy idealizes the entire Shcherbatsky family, in fact; and when he tells us that Levin is in love with all of them − 'encountering in them for the first time the home life of a cultured, honourable family of the old aristocracy, which Levin had been deprived of by the death of his own father and mother' (I, 6) − he is again drawing attention to an ideal of his own.

Next to the question of marriage and family, it is to the management of his estate that Levin's thoughts turn with most concern − and to that great fact of Russian life, which in the country it was impossible to overlook: the peasants. the two matters are related. A kind of peasant wisdom permeates *Anna Karenina*, and indeed a great deal of Tolstoy's writing less in the form of any distinct creed or philosophy than as a touchstone of which ideas and attitudes are close enough to the real condition of earthly existence to be valid. Levin notices that his housekeeper and his herdsman think he should be married. To have a wife and family has always seemed to him here on his estate a natural and necessary part of his wider calling in life, which is to find a just and productive way of working the land in cooperation with the peasants. When he finds himself with no hope of marrying Kitty and no desire to marry anyone else, Levin throws himself still more energetically into the task of managing his estate and finding a right relationship with the peasants; he even decides to write a book on the whole problem of agriculture in Russia. Tolstoy introduces again here many ideas and experiences of his own (these will be considered later), and brings Levin close to the conclusion that he had best simply take a peasant girl to wife. He is saved from pursuing this idea by a timely romantic coincidence in the plot. Doubtless the sophisticated reader will see in this too much of a Stendhalian contrivance, but the scene in which Levin changes his mind and realizes the true strength of his feeling for Kitty — which he must surely have rediscovered whenever he saw her again — is of such radiant realism, at once physically immediate and psychologically profound, that Tolstoy's imagination is clearly being stirred by something much more important than romance.

Tolstoy has few rivals in the difficult art of depicting experiences of spiritual revelation. He shows these occurring generally under the pressure of unusual bodily circumstances; they seem almost to be a vision of something in the external world, yet they are manifestly an excitement of heart and mind. And so it is in Levin's case: he has spent the night awake on a haycock, meditating on a day of hard, happy toil working side by side with his men; he is ready to renounce his 'useless education', eager to embrace the 'simplicity, integrity, and sanity' of a life of manual labour, uncertain only if the means to this end include marrying a peasant girl. '"All my old dreams of family life were nonsense, not the real thing", he told himself. "It's all ever so much simpler

and better"' (III, 12). Tolstoy evokes the precise character of
Levin's mood by describing how he reads confirmation of his
change of heart in the lovely sky above his head. And then he
sees Kitty pass in a coach, gazing out at the sunrise — and at
him. The sight of her causes all the resolutions he has made,
everything that had been stirring during that sleepless night,
to vanish — an effect of love which is at once like and yet
quite unlike the irresistible passion of Anna and Vronsky.
Thinking out other solutions to the dilemma of his life is a
mere second best, an artificial substitute for the real thing —
which for Levin, no less than for them, is the overwhelming
certainty, the palpable reality, of love. Tolstoy makes us feel
that Levin can feel and do otherwise as little as they can; the
force that drives them towards catastrophe must as surely
drive him in the end to marry Kitty. It feels, it looks, like a
force of nature. 'No', he said to himself, 'however good that
simple life of toil may be, I cannot go back to it. I love *her*'
(III, 12). He looks again at the sky and it has changed; the
cloud-shell he had delighted in earlier, and which seemed to
him the symbol of the ideas and feelings of the night, has
vanished too. Sometimes Tolstoy's symbolism is so firmly
grounded in the evident concreteness of a scene that it persuades us perfectly.

The scene in which Tolstoy meets Kitty again and proposes
to her is justly famous, and those who find it coy or sentimental may be overlooking the social and psychological realities
which have been built into it, and which make it
psychologically understandable (and not just whimsically
charming) that the lovers should communicate with one
another in the way they do. Levin has not ceased loving Kitty;
he still thinks of her in the same way, as the bride on whom
he has set his heart; it is impossible for him to imagine himself
talking to her for long about anything else — he is the kind
of man any other woman might be forgiven for finding a
bore. When they last met she refused him; although her sister
has since given him to understand that Kitty would not refuse
him again, he has long felt that he could not accept Dolly's
invitation to pay a visit on this understanding without

appearing to forgive, pity, and thus humiliate Kitty. How is he to cross the 'insuperable barrier' of her last rejection without reawakening painful memories or hurting her feelings — and indeed his own? Precisely the gap between them intensifies their feelings, compounded equally of joy and dread, and makes it especially hard for them to speak to one another. Neither of them takes any part in the general conversation, although the topics usually interest them; they are absorbed by a sense of silent converse between themselves. While the others argue, Levin and Kitty agree that arguments are due to people not saying the thing that really matters, which is a meaning behind the words, based on the basic likes and dislikes from which they spring. They are trying to show that they understand one another in several indirect ways, without actually starting an embarrassing and painful discussion about the past. They have in effect crossed the gap and now wish to remain in their new-found sense of togetherness in the present. So how shall they refer to the matter that has for so long stood between them? By communicating through a code of initial letters instead of spoken words, they show one another how intimately shared and intuitive is their mutual understanding; the fact that they can understand one another in this way answers all other questions. They invent a game in which both of them win. The difficult passage from private feeling to a proposal of marriage — especially difficult in their case — is rendered as easy and innocent as child's play (IV, 13).

That Kitty and Levin go through their wedding in a daze has already been observed; their behaviour and state of mind under the influence of their feelings is a largely humorous counterpart to the demonic helplessness of Anna and Vronsky. Yet there is seriousness too in Kitty's joyful distraction. Here again Tolstoy evokes the different situation of each sex. Kitty is aware of a new life beginning for her in much the same way that Anna was when her love for Vronsky was first consummated; the men do not experience the same kind of 'complete severance' from their past. The indifference Kitty feels towards the things, the habits the people she has loved and who have loved her horrifies her, at the same time that she rejoices at what has brought it about: a confusion of sentiment which echoes, though without tragic overtones, Anna's feelings – particularly with regard to her son. The problem for the men, which will have for Vronsky and Anna much more serious implications than for Levin and Kitty, is whether they will be able to preserve their 'freedom' after marriage – which means having an independent life of their own. When his bachelor friends taunt him about this on the eve of his wedding. Levin declares that he cannot conceive greater happiness than 'having no freedom whatever' (V, 2), but he has not been married long before he is exasperated at finding himself 'such a slave', and thinks, 'I ought to have been firmer and asserted my masculine independence' (V, 15). He is exasperated too by Kitty's preoccupation with trivial household matters:

Like all men, he had unconsciously pictured married life as the happy enjoyment of love, which nothing should be allowed to hinder and from which no petty cares should distract. He should, he thought, do his work and then rest from his labours in the happiness of love. His wife was to be beloved, and nothing more. But, like all men, he forgot that she too needed occupation.   (V, 14)

This difference soon becomes the occasion of quarrels between them. When he arrives home half an hour late from his work, she reproaches him: 'You go about enjoying yourself.' He, dissatisfied with himself because he sees that he has not been getting much done lately, reproaches her (silently): 'She has no real interests. She does not care about my work, or the estate, or the peasants, or music, though she's rather good at it, or reading. She does nothing and is quite content' (V, 15). Tolstoy resolves this gathering tension in two ways: most importantly, he points forward to the event which will change Kitty's life most profoundly, and which he saw, with Levin, as the ultimate meaning of marriage: 'She was preparing herself for the period of activity which was to come to her when she would be wife to her husband and mistress of the house, at the same time bearing, nursing, and bringing up her children.' Before considering the great event of Kitty's childbirth, we must look at the other way in which Tolstoy develops the relationship between Levin and Kitty. It is through an experience of death, which Tolstoy relates to birth — and introduces first.

Tolstoy has enriched the texture of the novel by giving to Levin a brother, Nikolay, and a half-brother, Sergey Ivanich Koznyshev. They make little difference to the plot — plot is relatively unimportant as an organizational principle of *Anna Karenina* — but they contribute considerably to the novel's realism and theme. It might be said crudely that their functions are, respectively, to die and to intellectualize; they provide opportunities for Levin to come to terms with these two fundamental experiences; they are part of his continuing education in the conflicting realities of life, which he is forever trying to reconcile in his mind. They are part therefore also of the total impression of realism made on the reader by the novel as a whole, part of the context, the entire frame of connections, to which every particular incident implicitly relates and from which it takes its meaning. Nikolay has always disturbed Levin's conscience by his radical views and refusal to live respectably, and even more because he embodies so inescapably, by virtue of being a brother with unbreakable ties of blood and memory, those basic facts of illness, misery, and death, which Levin finds so hard to assimilate. The mood of morbid pessimism to which Levin is prone feeds on the facts of Nikolay's tubercular condition; the thought of Kitty, by contrast, soon makes him forget all that, as Oblonsky jocularly observes. Levin wants to keep Kitty in a special compartment of his mind, where nothing disagreeable will touch her, partly in order to protect her and partly to protect himself. For her to become a real person, in his eyes and to herself, this has to change. Tolstoy skilfully places the incident of Nikolay's death just after the difficult first months of their marriage; it is one of the most important steps towards their better understanding of one another. The lesson is a very simple one: confronted with Nikolay dying in squalor, Levin does not know what to say or do, he is paralysed with horror and disgust. Kitty instinctively does know,

and immediately begins speaking to Nikolay 'in that unoffen-
ding sympathetic, gently animated way, natural to women'
(V, 17).

Since Tolstoy's time, the outlook implied by such a phrase
as 'natural to women' has met with resistance and resentment, even when it is meant, as here, as a tribute to a virtue
lacking in a man. Tolstoy is undeniably building up again
here a picture of sexual differences, on which rests his view
of the necessary domestic role that women have to play.
Women are good with invalids for the same reason that they
are good with children; they understand the mysteries of birth
and death, because they are physically involved with them, in
a way that men are not. And, in Tolstoy's view, understanding with no physical involvement, but with the mind alone,
is inevitably partial and inadequate, as we shall see later. The
realism of Kitty's development as a person is convincing only
in the light of these truths, if they are true, and so is the
inevitability of Anna's tragedy. Tolstoy's views on these
matters are not an occasionally intrusive addition to an otherwise realistic text, as critics sometimes argue. He would have
been the last person to teach an ideologically neutral reading
of the pure beauties of his or any other art. In idealizing
Kitty's behaviour at Nikolay's deathbed, he is trying to make
us feel what is ultimately most real in life, and how it has to
be responded to. Death is a great reminder of all that in life
defies reason, and the kind of reasoning mind Tolstoy
thought more typical of men is paralysed by not being able to
comprehend it; a girl like Kitty on the other hand, or Agatha
Mihailovna, Levin's uneducated housekeeper, has a positive
advantage in that she does not bother her head with unanswerable questions. Tolstoy did not intend this as praise
merely of ignorance, but rather of a simple religious faith,
which he, like Levin, found it hard to preserve in the face of
doubt. He is careful to stress that the care of women for the
dying and dead — it is they who lay out the corpse — is not
'instinctive, animal, and irrational', for they are concerned
not just to alleviate the sufferings of the body but also to
comfort and save the soul with religious rites. And he is

careful also to spell out that what they have is a kind of knowledge:

> [Levin] knew that many great and virile minds, whose thoughts on death he had read, had brooded over it and yet did not know one hundredth part of what his wife and Agatha Mihailovna knew . . . Both knew, without a shadow of a doubt, what sort of a thing was life and what death was, and though neither of them could have answered, or even have comprehended, the questions that presented themselves to Levin, they had no doubt of the significance of this event, and were precisely alike in their way of looking at it − a way they shared with millions of other people. The proof that they knew for a certainty the nature of death lay in the fact that they were never under an instant's uncertainty as to how to deal with the dying, and felt no fear. But Levin and others like him, though they might be able to say a good many things about death, obviously did not know anything about it, since they were afraid of death and had no notion what to do in the presence of death.   (V, 19)

It would not be hard to challenge Tolstoy's trust in 'knowledge' of this kind by thinking of examples in which confident behaviour and the agreement of others might be very poor evidence of truth. In the context of what is happening at this point in the novel, however, Levin's reflections appear completely convincing, as does Kitty's energetic, unsqueamish, and sensible treatment of Nikolay. The fact that she is not his close relative, whereas Levin is, should doubtless also be counted amongst the reasons for her undaunted behaviour and Nikolay's responsiveness; Tolstoy merely observes the positive effect on him of her charm and cheerfulness.

There is, of course, a further reason why Kitty comes into her own in this way, which has less to do with her religious faith and practical competence than with her uniqueness as a woman; this consists for Tolstoy in her destiny to bear children. Again the point is made by contrast with Levin's helpless male mind; he finds himself playing the same role of bumbling ineptitude and horrified incomprehension when Kitty is in labour; it is once more she who tries to reassure him. Tolstoy twice contrasts the basic destinies of a man and a woman 'in the dangerous and decisive moments of life' by means of a heroic simile, likening to a man's feelings before

battle what Kitty feels on two occasions in her life — just
before meeting Vronsky and then again at Nikolay's death. A
heroic image might have been even more appropriate for her
experience of childbirth, which proved to be more truly
'dangerous'. Tolstoy insists on the link between death and
birth by another of his coincidences in the plot: just when
Nikolay dies, Kitty's pregnancy is announced. The perspective throughout these sections of the novel, it should be
remembered, is Levin's rather than Kitty's; so the coincidence
is significant only for him — is, in fact, merely a coincidence
for him — and he would doubtless have perceived some deep
connection between these events whenever they had occurred.
In the long hours when Kitty is in labour, Levin recalls the
earlier occasion:

He only knew and felt that what was happening was similar to what
had happened a year ago at the deathbed in a provincial hotel of his
brother Nikolai. Only that had been sorrow, and this was joy. But
that sorrow and this joy were equally beyond the usual plane of
existence: they were like openings through which something sublime
became visible. And what was being accomplished now, as in that
other moment, was accomplished harshly, painfully; and in con-
templation of this sublime something the soul soared to heights it
had never attained before, while reason lagged behind, unable to
keep up.   (VII, 14)

In these great scenes of married life, in which first a death
takes place in the family and then the birth of a child, Tolstoy
achieves some of his most memorable realistic effects. His
style, like that of his contemporaries (in France especially),
becomes more naturalistic, in the sense that it dwells on the
physical and bodily process of experience beyond what is
required by the story. Indeed, beside these domestic events
Kitty and Levin have no other story. But the fact that in *Anna
Karenina* these ultimate experiences of life and of death, in
both their agonizing physical detail and also in their effect on
the mind, are represented as Levin's, sometimes objectively in
the sense simply that his actions constitute the guiding thread,
sometimes quite subjectively by recording what he thinks and
feels, lends to Tolstoy's realism its distinctively human and
persuasive quality. Though he dwells on the physical as

uncompromisingly as any naturalist writer, he does not betray the reader, as naturalism often does, into a detached and perverse enjoyment of physical effects for their own sake; these never exceed the spiritual awareness of the characters and in particular here of Levin. Even his frequently reiterated inability to understand what is going on as his brother slowly dies and his wife screams in pain, becomes a kind of eloquent testimony to some real meaning, and certainly some great mystery, in these events. The reader has the impression that he is sharing with Levin the experience of something too big and too bewildering to comprehend; even the failure of Tolstoy's style to do more than grope for words to say what that something truly is, becomes a strength rather than a weakness. The strain of language struggling to express the ineffable communicates the strain of Levin's actual experience in all its fits and starts. The association of womankind with the essential mystery of life, with the birth 'from some unknown realm' of individuals who then disappear through death back into the unknown, takes place in his mind; we learn little about the mysterious wisdom of woman beyond Levin's admiring incomprehension of it. The effectiveness of Tolstoy's realism is due to the way he makes us see what it is like to try and think these great ideas, rather than to his persuading us absolutely that they are true.

The picture of Kitty's and Levin's life together is filled out with many other detailed scenes and minor events, solidly connected in their domestic theme and their imaginative concreteness, but static and without the momentum of a story. The movement and growing tension of the novel derive from Anna's story, whose domestic life with Vronsky passes, on its fatal course towards tragedy, many points of experience which contrast with the settled existence of the Levins. Jealousy, for instance, which Anna calls her demon quite early in their relationship, soon comes between Kitty and Levin, but not for long. The amiable dandy who pays court to Kitty in her own home, because it seems to him the socially accepted role for a bachelor guest to play, finds himself turned out of the house. Levin's suspicion is unfounded, of course, and his reaction exaggerated, but Tolstoy has no doubt that Levin is really vulnerable; his realism is always alive to the significance even trivial things receive from feeling – from suspicion just as much as from love. How helpless the mind is to tell itself otherwise; far better, it seems here, to clear the air of this nuisance. And Kitty too is vulnerable; she is cleverer now than Levin and leads him to confess his blind susceptibility to Anna's demonic charm. Only Vronsky appears to be proof against such feelings; when Veslovsky, thrown out by Levin, goes to stay with Anna and Vronsky, the latter simply ignores the attentions which Anna attracts from this man as from so many others. Then there is the question of masculine independence and of a man's activities away from home; in a neatly handled contrast we see Levin and Vronsky setting out for the same purpose – to attend a meeting of local government. Vronsky is keen to go, for his energetic nature requires occupation; Anna as always is jealous and soon driven to call him back. Levin, by contrast, is reluctant to go, but Kitty encourages him. She is more confident of herself and of her role as mistress of her home to which many members of her large family now come, and where she will soon be a mother bringing up her own children. This is in striking contrast to Anna who is determined to have no more children in order not to spoil her beauty in which is all her trust.

The tragedy of Anna Arkadyevna Karenina

As a result of its origins in the theatre, the word tragedy connotes a story, focused on one person, and having a certain shape: it reaches a high point of good fortune, then falls under the weight not of unexpected misfortunes but of consequences implicit from the start. Anna's story has this shape. Its great fortunate moment comes when Anna lives with Vronsky in Italy: 'In that first period of her freedom and rapid return to health, she felt unpardonably happy and full of the joy of life' (V, 8). Only a few months elapse before she tries to tell Dolly of her new-found happiness:

'You look at me', she said, 'and wonder how I can be happy in my position? Well, I'm ashamed to confess it, but I . . . I am unpardonably happy. Something magical has happened to me; like suddenly waking up after a horrible, frightening dream and finding that your terrors are no more. I have woken up! I have lived through the agony and the misery, and now for a long while past, especially since we came here, I've been so happy! . . .' she said, looking at Dolly with a timid, questioning smile.   (VI, 18)

Alas, what she says is now no longer completely true, and Dolly is quick to discover the meaning of that smile, which like so many mute gestures and expressions in Tolstoy's narrative, communicates something else besides the spoken words. Anna needs reassurance, and she is close to tears when Dolly hastens to give it. What has happened in the meanwhile? What was indeed on the point of happening when not Anna, but Tolstoy, first used that phrase 'unpardonably happy', and used it twice, as though it contained some essential clue to her feelings? 'The desire for life, waxing stronger with recovered health, was so intense, and the conditions of life were so novel and delightful, that Anna felt unpardonably happy.' Tolstoy likewise describes Anna's state of mind by means of the same simile (of a dream) that Anna uses in speaking of herself − a rather rare endorsement by the author of a character's thoughts:

The memory of all that had happened after her illness − the reconciliation with her husband, the breach that followed, the news of Vronsky's wound, his sudden reappearance, the preparations for divorce, the departure from her house, the parting from her son − all seemed like some fevered dream from which she had wakened abroad and alone with Vronsky.   (V, 8)

Painful and slow is the descent of Anna's love into disaster. There are no sudden changes such as marked its upward surge; her life is slowly and irrevocably pulled apart. In her last hours, she is unable to imagine any life for herself at all; she finds herself standing over against life, seeing it in the pitiless glare of her utter isolation from it, with no further desire to participate, without sympathy or hope − not even for her own life, not even for herself. When she looks into a mirror, she momentarily does not recognize herself: a familiar literary device, which Tolstoy can use to particularly good effect, since it reminds us of that change and division in her identity which we have had occasion to comment on before; in her treatment of her husband, in her behaviour towards Vronsky, even in her understanding of herself, deep self-division has been a recurrent feature of her passion — under the stress of her domestic and social situation, needless to say — from the start. In the first crisis of her love 'she felt as though everything in her soul were beginning to be double, just as objects sometimes appear double to over-tired eyes' (III, 15). The image of waking from a dream has likewise a profound psychological appropriateness; it tells us of two states of mind between which there is a radical break. Might not Anna equally have said that now she lives in a dream of happiness after the painful realities she has endured? Tolstoy's realism perhaps means us to see that it is more natural for the healthy body to believe happiness is real, and to regard sufferings as nightmare. He repeatedly insists on Anna's recently recovered health as the bodily component of her joy in life; and when he twice says, and then has Anna say, that she is 'unpardonably happy', he is not so much expressing any remorse or sense of guilt as indicating her amazement that she can be feeling now as she does, that she can have left her old life so completely behind, as though in another state of existence, having no connection with her present one. 'Unpardonably' here is merely a way of saying 'completely and utterly', where one might have expected the painful realities of the past — which are indeed still realities, though not for her — to cast their shadow. It is, however, this unpardonable lack of connection which is the cause of her undoing.

The completeness of the rift shows itself at the simplest level in the matter of divorce. Looked at in the most matter-of-fact way — the way Stiva Oblonsky sees it — the reason why Anna is so wretched at home and in society is that she needs a divorce. Vronsky too, realizing that she suffers (though never fully understanding what she suffers), tries to persuade her that they must put an end to their unnatural situation. And this, as we have remarked, is from the beginning a prospect she cannot face; she dreads to think of losing her son and of her son's feelings towards her once he knows of her infidelity. She cannot contemplate divorce, but she can imagine blindly turning her back on the whole situation. If Vronsky 'were to say to her firmly, passionately, without a moment's hesitation, "Throw up everything and come with me!" then she would give up her son and go away with him' (III, 22). In the end, he does say something like that – being under the impression himself that the divorce has been agreed – and she does go with him. But she has still not got any nearer to accepting a divorce; with her brother's help preparations have evidently been made to obtain one, but she has refused it; more than ever she behaves as though there were no need for one. Eventually it falls to Dolly to try to persuade her to seek a divorce, as Stiva tried to persuade Karenin to grant one; there is, in fact, a greater complexity of situations and attitudes with regard to this one issue than with regard to any other in the novel – Karenin changes his mind on the matter five times. When Anna finally does agree to write to Karenin and ask him for a divorce, it is obvious that her heart is not in it; she is forced to make this move because she will otherwise not be able to accompany Vronsky to Moscow. But it is now too late.

Why does Anna refuse a divorce? Her reasons – or rather her deeply divided state of mind, her inability even to think about it, her recourse to morphine to forget – all come out during the course of her conversation with Dolly, to whom she says, speaking of her son and her lover,

I love these two beings only, and the one excludes the other. I cannot have them both; yet that is my one need. And since I can't have that, I don't care about the rest. Nothing matters; nothing, nothing!

(VI,24)

Doubtless her reasoning is not very rational, but it is never demeaning. Since she has already lost her son, and has no hope or intention of seeing him again, not even by another clandestine visit such as she once paid him on his birthday, one might think that a divorce could not now make the situation any worse. However, Anna is moved by proud self-respect not to wish to appeal to Karenin's generosity, by some emotional intransigence that cannot settle for the second best, and ultimately by a motive which she may not quite consciously think or feel, but which is embedded in the tone and force of Tolstoy's text. She begins to be touched by the momentum and menace of her own doom, to which she even alludes. Her friends beg her to avoid it by regularizing the situation she is already in, but she will not. She shows a kind of moral integrity and honesty by her recognition that nothing can ever put that situation right. She is in effect making a heroic stand; by refusing to compromise, by preferring to die rather than accept a flawed happiness, she assumes a tragic stance. To regularize her situation would be to agree to her loss of Seriozha, to endorse this loss, and to belittle it and herself. Beyond that, to seek divorce would be to betray her love for Vronsky by admitting that there is something wrong with it as it is, and this she has likewise always refused to do. Once, when Vronsky had challenged her with the question, 'For God's sake, which is better? To leave your child or keep up this degrading position?' Anna rebuked him:

'You say degrading . . . don't say that. Such words have no meaning for me . . . Try to understand that from the day I loved you everything, everything has changed for me. For me there is one thing, and one thing only − your love. If that's mine, I feel so uplifted, so strong, that nothing can be humiliating to me. I am proud of my position, because . . . proud of being . . . proud.' She could not say what she was proud of. Tears of shame and despair choked her. She stood still and sobbed.   (III, 22)

This is the very heroism of love and, while Tolstoy's moral intelligence knows that Anna's position is untenable, beyond explanation or justification, his imagination also responds to the pathos and passion of her role. In a similar exchange later, when Vronsky, wishing to remind her of her position and protect her from humiliation in public, warns her that she must not appear at the theatre, she replies,

'I don't care to know!' she almost shrieked. 'I don't care to. Do I regret what I have done? No, no, no! If it were all to do again, I should do just the same again. For us, for you and me, there is only one thing that matters, whether we love each other. Other people we need not consider. Why are we living apart here and not seeing each other? Why can't I go out? I love you, and nothing else matters to me so long as you have not changed', she said . . . glancing at him with a strange glitter in her eyes which he could not understand. 'Why don't you look at me?' (V, 32)

Tolstoy enhances the effect of Anna's refusal to compromise, and of her attempt to disregard social prejudice and live purely for Vronsky and for love, by means of various contrasting details in the picture he paints of society around her − beginning, as we have remarked, with the portrait of her husband, with his self-seeking concern for social position and propriety. Karenin typifies social affectation and falsity of feeling, and he is so lacking in passion, indeed in common human warmth and sympathy, that Anna's truly physical loathing for him communicates itself to the reader. Tolstoy makes his refusal to fight a duel, out of respect for his 'official duties', like his later refusal to grant a divorce, out of respect for 'Christian teaching', appear to be so much self-deceiving cant; how open and natural and generous Anna's passionate nature looks by comparison. It is the same in the scenes Tolstoy creates with Seriozha, who is told his mother is dead and who is being educated with an unfeeling lack of imagination, designed to repress − with painful success, to judge by a later scene − his spontaneous emotional nature too; he would be ready enough to love her still, we feel, if only he were allowed to. Most striking of all are the repeated references to the way adulterous relationships are carried on and condoned generally in this society. 'She did what everyone else does . . . only they hide it', remarks the only society lady renowned for plain speaking. 'She couldn't be deceitful, and she did a fine thing' (VII, 20). Anna is understandably outraged that Betsy Tverskoy − 'la femme la plus dépravée qui existe' − who once thought Anna's liaison with Vronsky entertaining, and whose salon is notorious for fashionable intrigues (including her own), should now say she does not care to know her so long as her position is 'irregular'. Doubtless Anna remembers very well the kind of thing she used to hear from Betsy: for instance, about another

woman unfaithful to her husband. Anna could not understand what part the husband played. 'The husband? . . . As
you know, in decent society one doesn't talk of certain details
of the toilet. That's how it is with this.' And Betsy continues:

'I understand you, and I understand Liza. Liza's one of those naive
creatures who no more understand the difference between right and
wrong than a child. At least, she did not understand it when she was
very young. And now she's aware that the role of not understanding
suits her. Now, perhaps, she doesn't know on purpose', said Betsy
with a faint smile. 'Still, it suits her, just the same. You see, you can
look at a thing tragically and turn it into a misery, or you can take
it simply and even humorously. Possibly you are inclined to look on
the tragic side.'
   'How I wish I knew other people as I know myself!' Anna said
gravely and thoughtfully. 'Am I worse than others, or better?
Worse, I think.'   (III, 17)

   Once again, Anna voices a thought which is on the reader's
mind, and presumably also on the author's, as though
Tolstoy were not merely thinking about her but also through
her. She does not understand the way the world behaves, she
cannot conduct her love affair with the insouciance of her
brother or the members of Betsy Tverskoy's set: does this
make her better than they are or worse? We do not have to
decide the matter in these terms: she is both better and worse,
she is greater, and her fate is tragic, whereas theirs is trivial.
If she just wanted to flirt with, or even sleep with, Vronsky,
society would wink; even Karenin would have been 'prepared
to allow those relations to be resumed, provided the children
were not disgraced, that he was not deprived of them or
forced to change his attitude' (IV, 20). Karenin, however,
feels helpless; he finds that everyone is against him, and
knows that he will not be allowed to do 'what seemed to him
now so natural and right'. The scene is a crucial one, heavy
with the fatality Karenin thinks of as 'a brutal force that guid-
ed life against his spiritual inclinations'. He has been deeply
touched, and for the first time in his life, by Anna's desire for
reconciliation with him when she thought she was dying; and
he is the kind of man, for all his faults, to cherish and sustain
such an experience. He will make the greatest concessions

now, even listening to Oblonsky as he persuades him, against his conscience, to agree to a divorce — which Anna also does not want. Karenin too only asks to be allowed to love Anna and her newborn child. So who or what is against him, against them both — what is the brutal force? It is partly, no doubt, the efforts of insensitive people to insist on a socially acceptable solution. But it is partly also Anna's return to health, and to her old physical vitality and temperament and emotional need. 'The sight of him has a physical effect on me, it puts me beside myself. I can't, I can't live with him' (IV, 21). Anna's tragedy is rooted somewhere deep within herself, in her own nature, and she knows it: 'I'm lost, lost! Worse than lost! . . . It's not ended yet . . . but the end will be terrible.' At this stage, her husband, her family, her friends, society at large are all ready to be accommodating; it is she who cannot accommodate herself to the reality of her situation. Her very integrity forbids it, her wholeness as a person.

A lesser nature might have avoided such extremes of feeling, or simply enjoyed the distraction of a love affair, as her brother does, with his easy-going 'philosophy' of taking the good with the bad. From the moment Anna first returns home after her meetings with Vronsky, she is riven with tension: 'She felt her nerves being stretched more and more tightly, like strings round pegs . . . she was afraid every minute that something within her would snap under the intolerable strain' (I, 29). Then the tension had been not at all unpleasant, but rather overwhelmed her with joy. Now she knows it will destroy her: 'I'm like an over-strained violin string that must snap' (IV, 21). For her there is no half-way state between complete integrity and complete destruction. Even when she escapes from the intolerable tension of a life divided between her husband and her lover, new tensions grow between herself and Vronsky. All have to do with his role and activity in the world; so intense is her desire to keep him totally to herself that any interests which take him away from her she regards as a threat. Already during their first days together Anna 'dreaded nothing so much as losing his love, though she had no grounds for fearing this'. He, on the

other hand, 'soon began to feel that the realization of his
desires brought him no more than a grain of sand out of the
mountain of bliss he had expected' (V, 8). Tolstoy has a keen
eye for the effect on them of their social situation, first
abroad, then in Petersburg, and after that on Vronsky's
country estate; it is always Vronsky who is in need of occupation, and he who is concerned for his position in society and
for hers, which she wilfully ignores, until he becomes as
exasperated at the embarrassment she causes him as Karenin
had been. But these, of course, are mere secondary causes of
what goes wrong between them; they are more in the nature
of effects from that primary cause, which is the deep division
introduced into her life by love − and by her own nature,
which is too fine to tolerate such division.

There are other secondary causes besides, which in the end
degenerate into senseless suspicions and irritations. Tolstoy
also sees again here how very unequally placed a man and a
woman are, especially in a situation like this, where it is
inevitable that they will think and feel quite differently. Anna
is materially altogether dependent on Vronsky, as she had
formerly been on Karenin, a dependence which Tolstoy
stresses on a number of occasions when she is in need of
money, and instinctively tries to refuse it. In their last dark
days together, when Anna has started to brood over all the
cruel words Vronsky might have spoken to her − 'and unmistakably wanted to say' − as well as those he actually has
said, she puts the following brutal phrases into his mouth:
'"Return to your husband then! If you need money, I'll give
it to you. How much do you want?" . . . She could not
forgive him these words any more than if he had actually said
them' (VII, 26). The parallelism within the novel is effective
again here, reminding us for instance of how wretchedly
Dolly is at the financial mercy of Stiva; even Kitty felt at a
disadvantage during the first months of her marriage − until
the birth of her first child. Anna, we recall, has decided to
have no more children, in order to keep her looks, and be 'the
friend and companion of her husband'. She reads seriously
and takes an interest in all his projects − the very thing Levin

expected of Kitty — but Tolstoy notes that 'her chief pre-occupation was herself, and how far she was dear to Vronsky, how far she could compensate to him for all he had given up' (VI, 25). The implied moral criticism of her here, and earlier during Dolly's visit, for having 'devoted so much care to her appearance', seems bitterly unfair. What else, what more, could Anna do? Tolstoy's moral insight is not one of blame, however, and even less is it one of prejudiced comment on a situation we might otherwise feel has nothing very grievously wrong with it. There is everything wrong with Anna's posi-tion: 'He has the right to go when and where he chooses. Not simply to go away, but to leave me. He has all the rights, while I have none' (VI, 32). And her reflections bring her back to the prospect she is least able to face. There is one solution to the dilemma of having to hold him by means of her love and charm, and that is 'not to hold him . . . but to become so bound up with him, to be in such a position that he could not abandon her. That solution was divorce and marriage.' For her who has believed in the power of love alone, it is like a confession of failure to have to think of holding Vronsky by marital ties. Nor will she ever do so; instead Anna makes out of the struggle for his love a death agony for both of them.

The concluding chapters of their life together make sombre reading. Tolstoy's imagination is always alive to the emotional components of a situation, and these are now a witches' brew of jealousy, suspicion, resentment, despera-tion, pride, and much besides, which he calls simply an evil spirit. 'The irritability which kept them apart had no tangible cause . . . It was an inner irritation, grounded in her mind on the conviction of a decline in his love for her; in his, on regret that for her sake he had placed himself in a difficult position . . . Each thought the other in the wrong and seized every op-portunity to prove it' (VII, 23). Small cause for tragedy, one might think, yet how profoundly Tolstoy comprehends the disaster that may be forged out of the merest scraps of daily intercourse. Anna and Vronsky see with loveless eyes the bare bones of the relationship with which they began. He is for her now no more than the womanizer we glimpsed — though she did not — at the beginning, before their great love transformed him; and what had that been, she wonders, but a triumph for his vanity? What had her love ever been but desire to enjoy the effect of her beauty? She measures his love for her by the intensity and completeness of the passion she is able to inspire; and now, as she is forced to tell herself (in English), 'the zest is gone'. She is not so much jealous — her suspicions are trumped up for emotional effect — as 'unsatisfied'. She is unable to imagine 'any new feeling' between Vronsky and herself; she does not want to be treated 'kindly and gently out of a sense of *duty*' — she does not, she discovers now, even want to be married to him: 'If I could be anything but his mistress, passionately caring for nothing but his caresses — but I can't, and I don't want to be anything else' (VII, 30). Her suicide is not the expression purely of despair but, like all her earlier threats, is aimed at Vronsky; it is the last throw of her passion, it is meant to affect him for ever so that he will never forget her. Tolstoy repeatedly mentions one detail of Vronsky's appearance — is it a physical trait or a spiritual one? — which always irritated Anna: his self-possession. For her it means that he does not love her, or not enough. Her last desperate will is to destroy that, together with herself; and she surely does.

Ideas and beliefs

It is one of the most remarkable features of *Anna Karenina*, and certainly a decisive element of its greatness, that it contains as much depth of thought as depth of passion; it is a novel not only of love but of ideas. Tolstoy achieves this intellectual interest without in any way damaging or departing from his realist vision. He rarely displays ideas in the abstract, or in philosophical reflections of his own (though he did, at various times, personally subscribe to many of the ideas expressed by Levin). Ideas are lodged in the minds of his characters, as well as more generally in their lives, where what they think both has a real effect upon their experience and is also affected by their experience — by things that happen to them, by their situation, their temperament, and so on. Levin is the novel's intellectual hero, as Anna is its heroine of love, and his thoughts are portrayed under the stress of circumstances which are every bit as concrete and intense as any that surround her feelings. The wisdom of the novel, if it is possible to talk in such terms, consists in discovering the whole truth about particular thoughts as well as about particular emotions: what thoughts and emotions in effect are in relation to the personal and social and physical context — the 'reality' — which fiction presents to the imagination.

It is this imaginative context of the novel, its highly composite realism, which supports a crucial distinction in Tolstoy's thinking; that between merely cerebral ideas, or opinions, and ideas that are truly lived, or beliefs. In the anguish of his brother's dying and of Kitty's labour, Levin prays with evident fervour; at other times he thinks that he does not believe. Tolstoy is not trying to persuade us simply that one activity comes closer to truth than the other. Doubtless he has, like any imaginative writer, a preference for scenes where something happens, where reality is vivid, where the moment brims over; the prejudice of reason in favour of detached reflection, in which the mind is in contact with nothing more real than its own ideas, runs counter to the preferences of the imagination. But moments of religious awareness and prayer form only one, rather intermittent strand in Levin's experience, and Tolstoy appeals in a much more subtle way to the credibility of Levin's spiritual pilgrimage as a whole. The truth of Levin's ideas is in the first place imaginative and artistic, and not essentially different from the truth of other kinds of experience in the book, by which we are convinced (or not) on literary grounds. We may believe in him, without necessarily believing what he believes. Indeed, he himself has much more faith in the totality of his life, just the way it is, than in anything he can say or think about it. When his moment of revelation comes, he cannot tell Kitty, because he cannot put it into words. Tolstoy sketches the kind of thoughts which pass through Levin's head, but he makes clear, partly by the sketchiness of the thoughts, that they are not the revelation itself; the final two paragraphs are remarkable chiefly for the realism of his recognition that his life will probably go on much the same. Besides the things Levin mutters about God and the soul, what he appears to have glimpsed is a truth implicit already in his search for the truth, a truth embodied in the way he lives, and ultimately in the person he is.

It is as though he had caught a glimpse of himself from the outside − and seen himself as Kitty sees him, for instance. We have already had occasion to note the advantage she enjoys in Tolstoy's eyes, just because she is a woman and also not an intellectual. She has never been impressed by his religious doubts (she is more disturbed by what he confesses − inconsiderately, as Tolstoy observes, for 'he had not put himself in her place' − about the lusts of his body). 'Through her love she knew his whole soul, and in his soul she saw what she wanted.' This might be no more than the blindness of love or inexperience; Tolstoy's realism is at its strongest when it perceives but does not decide such things. 'She was firmly persuaded that he was as much a Christian as herself, and indeed a far better one; and that all that he said about it was just one of his funny masculine freaks, like his jest about her *broderie anglaise*' (V, 19). Now that, surely, must be a bit of girlish light-mindedness? But then she challenges him with quite penetrating shrewdness, when he pretends to be dissatisfied with his own inadequacies; she knows that he is too happy to be altogether sincere (VI, 3). And in the end this is what Levin himself also comes to understand. He keeps going off by himself and brooding on the great unanswerable questions of life and death and the soul, but Kitty, though she used to be quite alarmed, smiles now when she thinks of his scepticism, and calls him funny. She knows his good heart, his dread of hurting anyone's feelings, even a child's: 'With him it's everything for others, nothing for himself.' Levin also reflects on his own behaviour and discovers in it an important lesson for himself:

It was as impossible not to look after the interests of his brother and sister, and of all the peasants who came to him for advice and were accustomed to do so, as it is impossible to fling down a child one is carrying in one's arms. Then he had to see to the comforts of his sister-in-law and her children, whom he had invited to stay with them, and of his wife and baby, and it was impossible not to spend a portion of each day with them.

And all this, together with shooting and his new hobby of beekeeping, filled up that life of his which seemed to him to have no meaning at all when he began to think about it.   (VIII, 10)

The lesson is quite simply this: 'He had been living rightly, but thinking wrongly.'

If the lesson Levin learns is put into words, it sounds rather confusing and confused. In part it is a denial of the possibility of formulating truth; in part it is an assertion of innate moral knowledge; and in part it is an affirmation of traditional religious and moral belief: 'It was clear to him that he could only live by virtue of the beliefs in which he had been brought up.' But as he ruminates on what the Church actually teaches, nothing very clear comes to mind. Levin reduces the entire teaching of the Church to one very general idea:

At the back of every article of faith of the Church could be put belief in serving truth rather than one's personal needs. And each of these dogmas not only did not violate that creed but was essential for the fulfilment of the greatest miracles, continually manifest upon earth — the miracle that made it possible for the world with its millions of individual human beings, sages and simpletons, children and old men, everyone, peasants, Lvov, Kitty, beggars and kings, to comprehend with certainty one and the same truth and live that life of the spirit, the only life that is worth living and which alone we prize.
                                                                    (VIII, 13)

The style of this sentence, the sheer distribution of the words, makes it rather hard to see what truth is meant or what the miracle is. The miracle is perhaps that there is a truth, and that men are united in their certainty that there is one. Does it matter very much what men think it is? 'When Levin puzzled over what he was and what he was living for, he could find no answer and fell into despair; but when he left off worrying about the problem of his existence he seemed to know both what he was and for what he was living . . . When he did not think, but just lived, he never ceased to be aware of the presence in his soul of an infallible judge who decided which of two possible courses of action was the better and which the worse' (VIII, 10). That was before his revelation, which rescued him from doubt and suicide. In fact, he believes much the same thing afterwards, with the difference that he now feels it to be miraculous that he has this belief and shares it with all men — with all believing men, that is, for mere thinking men are sure to miss the point, as he had done. Levin tells himself that he formerly failed to find any answer to the great question of life's meaning and purpose, because 'reason is incommensurable with the problem'. However, his new-found faith still depends rather considerably on the kind of thinking he pretends to reject. The reason why mankind's moral awareness strikes him as miraculous is that he thinks it is something the materialist account of existence cannot explain:

What it is we should live for and what is good: that is the only knowledge I and all men possess that is firm, incontestable, and clear, and it cannot be explained by reason — this knowledge is outside the sphere of reason, it has no causes and no effects . . . Here is a miracle, the one possible, everlasting miracle, surrounding me on all sides, and I never noticed it! . . . Reason discovered the struggle for existence, and the law demanding that I should strangle all who hinder the satisfaction of my desires. That is the deduction of reason. But loving one's neighbour reason could never discover, because it's unreasonable.   (VIII, 12)

Levin's thoughts are recognizably of his time, though he may well be right in believing that he is addressing a problem which is perennial; certainly the relationship of individual consciousness to bodily existence, and more particularly the identification of individuality with moral independence, are matters which continue to exercise the Western conscience more than a century after Tolstoy wrote. Philosophically, his reflections are obviously rather scrappy and doubtless not of much interest in themselves; but if, as we have suggested, their claim on our attention is much more literary and imaginative than philosophical, then this is in keeping with their message. The novel is appealing to a special kind of evidence of its own. In one sense, its claim is a large one: to go beyond philosophy altogether. Levin is represented as having kept abreast of materialist thinking in his day, and as having turned, in dissatisfaction with its dusty answers, to Plato, Spinoza, Kant, Schelling, Hegel, and Schopenhauer. This too has been a failure — not surprisingly perhaps with a mind capable of substituting the word *love* for the word *will* in Schopenhauer's philosophy and feeling quite cheered up 'for a day or two' — and so has his study of Khomyakov's doctrine of the Church. The concepts of the philosophers strike him as being verbal traps, and their speculations as no more substantial than a house of cards. His touchstone is 'life', and the whole authority of Tolstoy's realism vouches now for his conviction that here is a truth greater than mere words.

Where the greatest meditations of Western philosophy have failed to move him, two phrases spoken by an old peasant act on Levin with the force of a revelation: 'He thinks of his soul. He does not forget God' (VIII, 11). Levin's imagination is suddenly seized by the realization of how extraordinary it is that a man, any man, should actually say such a thing. For the peasant is speaking, with unquestioning certainty, of a reality that cannot be seen — a reality that is not separate from the visible and tangible, but complements and transforms it. These few words are not so much an answer to Levin's questions, as an indication that the world is a different kind of place from what he had thought, and life a different kind of experience. The peasant has been working side by side with Levin, who has been trying as usual to get his men to operate the machines correctly, and has ended up doing the job himself, while through his mind the big unanswered questions run: 'What am I? Why am I here? What is all this being done for?' These are, as we know from earlier occasions, just the sort of circumstances in which Levin most readily feels reconciled, and most in contact with the life that reassures him. The sheer physicality of the experience is important, the dust and sweat, the basic work on the soil to produce food, the conversation with simple and unaffected men: all this is real. But something else is needed to turn this commonplace reality, which a moment before had appeared to Levin dreary and senseless, into a radiant vision of life. It is something which happens in Levin's heart and mind, and it is out of all proportion to the literal sense of the words he has heard; Tolstoy deliberately makes these very brief, and whether deliberate or not, the inadequacy of Levin's subsequent philosophizings has the effect of pointing towards something much greater than themselves: 'I have discovered nothing. I have simply opened my eyes to what I already knew. I have come to the recognition of that force that not only in the past gave me life but now too gives me life.' Tolstoy quickly sketches a scene with the children, who misbehave without understanding what they are doing; it is an obvious yet effective parable, and provides him with a good phrase to describe the failure, common to all human beings, to realize what life is: 'They could not take in the magnitude of all they habitually enjoyed' (VIII, 13).

To understand the magnitude of the reality we live by and in, the reality we are — and the Russian word *ob'yom* means quite concretely the volume and size, and *pol'zovat'sya* means enjoy in the embodying sense in which one enjoys opportunities or privileges — might stand as a definition of what Tolstoy's realism aims at and achieves. Many other ideas in the novel are made to appear small and trivial as a result of being exposed in such large and substantial surroundings — rather as Karenin's bureaucratic notions fall like a flimsy bridge as the emotional abyss of Anna's infidelity opens before him. The ideas of Levin's intellectualizing half-brother Koznyshev, for example, appear inadequate because he never considers fully what they mean in reality. He is interested in 'the fashionable question whether there was a dividing line between the psychological and the physiological phenomena in human activity', but when Levin bluntly asks him what will happen to his own soul at death, Koznyshev blandly dismisses the question. He appears in much the same light at the end of the book, when he is preaching the cause of Slav solidarity against the Turks. His idea that the entire people are possessed by the same feeling seems to echo

Levin's enthusiasm for the perennial spiritual certainty which unites all men; but Tolstoy at once highlights the difference – Levin asks a peasant what he thinks, and the idea of Slav solidarity clearly means nothing to him. Nor to Levin himself, who declares: 'I'm one of the people myself, and I don't feel it.' Political ideas altogether tend to come off badly in the novel, partly through their association also with Karenin, and largely, of course, because Levin tends to find them unreal. The persuasiveness of this kind of personal honesty, which judges ideas by their emotional significance in the context of his own experience, depends heavily for its effect on his commanding position as hero in the novel; naturally, where the hero is, there is the centre and standard of the real. Trusting to this effect, Tolstoy continues to support Levin throughout the political scenes, in which even his incomprehension and ineptitude serve to discredit the institution of local government – which, of course, Koznyshev advocates; Levin's response appears to be the genuine one, while the others look as if they are engaged in some sort of charade. Of Koznyshev's zeal for public causes Levin wonders, evidently like his author, whether 'it was not so much a quality as a lack of something' (III, 1).

Where Levin has theoretical ideas of his own, on the subject of the right way to farm the land, these too are subtly discredited, though his personal integrity and actual practice never are. Tolstoy's technique is to allow life, in the shape simply of events and personalities, to thwart Levin's theories. First he aspires to better managerial control; but the experience of working alongside the peasants changes all that. He realizes there is an irreconcilable disparity of interests: 'He was fighting for every farthing of his share, whereas they were only anxious to be left to do their work lazily and comfortably' (III, 24). For a while he loses interest in the whole question, partly as a result of his unexpected encounter again with Kitty – in the scene which so suddenly and dramatically changes his ideas about marriage. When discussions with his neighbours revive his agricultural ideas, he tries to argue his way beyond their conflicting liberal and conservative opinions, and arrives at a new theory: cooperatives – which allow the peasants to work in whatever way is natural to them, but encourage them with the prospect of shared profits. His neighbours argue for the sake of argument, and Levin realizes that for them ideas have no connection with actual practice. With him it will be different, he will lead a bloodless revolution, write a book . . . The reader notices the contrast between the experience which inspires this idea – a visit to a peasant smallholding, which is worked by the family which owns it – and the outcome: Levin excitedly dreaming of himself as the social saviour of Russia. Needless to say, his own peasants, whom he does not dream of making the owners of his land, do not cooperate. He is misunderstood on all sides. His housekeeper misinterprets him, supposing he is working for the good of his soul, and then telling him that what he really needs is a wife. His brother Nikolai accuses him of trying to hedge between communism and existing forms of land-ownership: 'You want to show that you are not simply exploiting the peasants, but have some idea in mind' (III, 32). And to research his ideas further, but with a strong suggestion that in fact he is running away from this and other problems, Levin leaves the country altogether on a foreign tour. Later in the novel, even good-natured Oblonsky revives the attack on Levin's ideas, accusing him of being a hypocrite. Typical of his class, Levin dislikes the new-rich entrepreneurs, and he has sharp opinions about the evil of money made by capitalist speculation: 'All profit that is out of proportion to the labour expended is dishonest' (VI, 11). We might expect Tolstoy to share this view, which accords with Levin's enthusiasm for physical toil shoulder to shoulder with his men; but he does not allow it to prevail here. Oblonsky, who is as much the frank, self-interested realist in matters of money as of sex, and is after a well-paid position with one of the new businesses, has no difficulty in putting Levin down. For does not Levin derive far more wealth from working his estate than any of his peasants enjoy? Would he ever consider giving his land to them? He is forced to admit that he can be just 'only negatively, in the sense that I don't try to increase the difference that exists between my position and theirs'.

Not that Oblonsky's views are to be thought of here or anywhere else as particularly admirable; Tolstoy trivializes him to the end, by showing his pleasure at getting (by graft) the job he wanted — with no mention of any grief at his sister's suicide. As for brother Nikolay's ideas, these are submerged by the various very strong emotional effects which this man's wretched bodily condition and way of life arouse in Levin and Kitty and the reader. The last thing we are likely to think about in his regard is the validity of his doctrines; nor is this treatment, though extreme in degree, unique in kind, or designed merely to dispose of a social revolutionary. The truth is rather that at no point in the novel does Tolstoy seek to make ideas as such prevail with the reader. In the scene in which Oblonsky argues with Levin, we hear much more than an exchange of ideas. The mood of the three men, relaxing away from home after a day's shooting, the tensions between them, Levin's stifled dislike of the brash bachelor who has been flirting with Kitty, the 'covert antagonism between the brothers-in-law, as if the fact of their being married to sisters had provoked rivalry as to who had ordered his life best' — these are some of the physical and psychological constituents of their discussion, and they convince the reader quite as much as the rightness of anyone's ideas. And it ends, as discussions do in life, with nothing proved and nothing changed, but with the participants going their different ways, behaving in accordance with their character, being themselves. Tolstoy achieves one of his typically lifelike and persuasive effects as Levin drifts off to sleep, his mind filled by noises and snatches of conversation from outside the barn by thoughts of shooting early on the morrow, and lastly by recollections of the recent discussion. Perhaps Oblonsky was right in his criticisms of him . . . 'Well, it can't be helped' (VI, 11). Levin is beginning to see and accept himself the way he is; he does not need to prove himself or his ideas; he is married now and contented. And we accept him too, seeing his greater integrity and independence by comparison with his friends, who have gone off to flirt with the peasant girls. We have in such moments a very realistic sense, which is to say a very composite and composed one, of the place of ideas in the life of the whole man. And where else but in the lives of men do ideas have any reality at all?

As Levin's life becomes more fulfilled, more full simply of family cares and family happiness, the management of his estate, though a part of these, cannot be his sole concern, and his theoretical and philosophical preoccupations diminish:

These things occupied him now, not because he justified them to himself by any sort of general principles, as he had done in former days; on the contrary, disenchanted as he was on the one hand by the failure of his earlier efforts for the general welfare, and too much occupied on the other with his own thoughts and the mass of business with which he was burdened from all sides, he had completely abandoned all considerations of public weal and busied himself with all this work for no other reason than because it seemed to him that he must do what he was doing – that he could not do otherwise.   (VIII, 10)

What had appealed to him formerly, in all his work for the good of humanity, for Russia, for the province, for the village as a whole, had been 'the idea'; the activity itself had been clumsy, 'incoherent', and he had never been convinced of its absolute necessity. He realizes soon after he has married how the context of his work has changed and with that its significance: 'Formerly this work had been an escape from life; he used to feel that without it life would be too gloomy' (V, 15). Now he thinks he needs it 'so that life might not be too uniformly bright' – which is almost another way of saying that he does not need it at all. The reader soon begins to realize that no further reforms are proposed for Levin's estate and that his book will never be written. Were he not so contentedly busy, his state of mind might give cause for alarm; for Levin takes refuge in a social situation he can neither justify nor change, and in a kind of residual religious faith which he cannot think out. The self-evidently right order of life, in which he puts his trust, surely cannot continue much longer on such a basis – so at least a modern reader is likely to feel, with historical hindsight. But, while the men and minds of Levin's generation were evidently at risk, just this

state of mind, stretched between the certainties of an older
social and cultural order and the uncertainties and doubts of
a newer one, may have been extraordinarily advantageous for
Tolstoy the writer. He was in a position perhaps to enjoy the
best of both worlds.

Tolstoy is able to go very far in the direction, fashionable
in his day, of a naturalistic portrayal of inner experience,
showing ideas and beliefs to be inextricably bound up with
physiological conditions, yet without forgetting that man
'must live for his soul'. The body-based psychology which introduces Oblonsky in chapter I is maintained until the end of
the novel, carrying with it the unspoken implication that
thinking is not in itself quite natural to man, and certainly not
an independent, nor even a dominant activity. When Kitty
meets the pious people at the German spa, we are made to
understand very plainly that she is being taken in, and why.
After her experience with Vronsky, she wants to escape from
fashionable society and from thoughts of love and marriage,
perhaps even from her own nature. And here now is 'a completely new world . . . a world that had nothing in common
with her past, an exalted, noble world, from the heights of
which she could contemplate her past calmly' (II, 33). She enjoys playing the role of sister of mercy, without realizing how
much of the effect she produces is due simply to her prettiness
and charm. Her father, incarnation of the stout Russian
virtues of good-humour and honest common sense, soon
brings her back to earth: he disabuses her about the main lady
invalid: the only thing wrong with her, he reveals, is that her
legs are too short − she finds being bed-ridden more becoming. By a series of deft touches, Tolstoy also dispels the
mysterious aura which surrounds the long-suffering Varenka
who attends this invalid: she is socially disadvantaged and
physically somewhat limp − she lives 'by principles', whereas
Kitty lives, as she says, 'by my own heart'. Varenka is one of
nature's victims, and the scene in which she and Koznyshev
fail to get engaged to one another discredits them both. Kitty,
by contrast, gets her man − or another one when the first
fails her. For her, love is so physically consuming that

disappointment makes her body ill; but by the same token her body is strong enough to revive. Again here, Tolstoy shows her father's old-fashioned good sense, at the expense of the foolish and deceitful theories of doctors.

Religious enthusiasm is made to appear even more eccentric in the scenes which show Karenin's flight into piety and the emotional wiles of Lydia Ivanovna. Karenin is seeking solace from his failure with Anna, which he might otherwise be forced with her return to health, to see as basically physical and sexual; and he also does not want to acknowledge that his career is faltering or that he is an object of derision amongst the robust and successful: '"How strong they all are, how physically sound . . . It is truly said that all is evil in the world", he thought, with another sidelong glance at the calves of the gentlemen of the bedchamber' (V, 24). Although formerly he had disliked Lydia's ecstatic fervour, he now swallows her doctrine of salvation for the elect few: 'It was so essential to him in his humiliation to have some elevated standpoint, however imaginary, from which, looked down on by all, he could look down on others, that he clung to this delusion of salvation as if it were the real thing' (V, 22). Lydia resembles Karenin in her capacity for self-deception: deserted by a dissipated husband — seeking solace from her? — she enjoys sanctimoniously imposing on Karenin, his son, and his household, and of course, with an obvious kind of cruel satisfaction, on Anna. Tolstoy's characteristic sureness of touch in regard to his characters' physical nature provides two further details: it is said of Lydia that she had never been able to understand what it was that led women astray, and also that emotional agitation induces in her attacks of asthma. The effect of having Anna's divorce hang in the balance of Lydia's latest superstition, her trust in a clairvoyant charlatan, which she has foisted on Karenin too, along with more conventional cant, is to destroy any vestiges of respect in the reader for the kind of social prejudices which are making Anna's life impossible. Whatever virtue Tolstoy saw in family life, and whatever evil he saw in divorce, had for him absolutely nothing to do — this he goes out of his way to make clear — with the false emotions and affected lives of Lydia Ivanovna's circle. The moral law which explains the inevitability of Anna's tragedy resides less in the chimeras of such people's minds than in her own passionate personality and experience.

In the great scenes of spiritual exaltation, which Anna goes through, we do not for one moment suspect her of false feeling, any more than we suspect her of mere flirtatiousness in her love for Vronsky. Her spiritual realizations are so substantial, so entirely one with her whole person, with her imagination, and with the reality surrounding her that they cannot properly be described as either ideas or beliefs. Tolstoy's description of the absence in Lydia Ivanovna and Karenin of any genuine belief shows what he thought genuineness of soul consists in: 'Like Lydia Ivanovna and others who shared her views, Karenin was quite devoid of that spiritual capacity in virtue of which conceptions springing from the imagination become so real that they demand to be made conformable with other conceptions and with reality itself' (V, 22). On one occasion Karenin does achieve this fullness or reality of response, and it is Anna who inspires it in him. She believes she is dying, she is drugged and delirious, and she begs Karenin to forgive her; she declares she is now her real and essential self — *nastoyashchaya* suggests abiding or permanent — and also that she is now entire and whole (*vsya*), a word which recalls by contrast the sense of division evoked by her love affair (IV, 17). Karenin is moved by her emotion, a movement he has in the past always resisted in himself (the *rasstroistvo* he feels is strong agitation, distraction, upset, and the opposite of the ordered mentality he tries to maintain). When he accepts this emotional disturbance of his official persona, this emotion which Anna has caused in him, he discovers 'a happiness he had never known. He was not thinking that the Christian law which he had been trying to follow all his life enjoined him to forgive and love his enemies; yet a glad feeling of love and forgiveness filled his heart.' The gesture of forgiveness she then further inspires him to make towards Vronsky produces an effect of quite devastating power. Whether this is to be regarded as an effect of Tolstoy's artistic presentation, or a real-life effect – to be admired, that is to say, on moral or on aesthetic grounds – is a question obviously impossible to answer. In such moments Tolstoy's moral realism can be seen to be doing – like all great literature – something quite different from mirroring reality; it creates a reality in its own image. We are not looking at a more or less imaginative idea of real events, but imaginatively living through events which are ideas. Reading realistically, we feel how Vronsky is spiritually devastated; the spineless husband whom he has despised now destroys him by his moral magnanimity more surely than by any duel he might have fought. Vronsky shoots himself out of mortified humiliation rather than out of sorrow for the loss of Anna's love.

In the intensity and integrity of her spiritual life Anna is after all comparable with Levin; across the gap separating their two stories, one experience unites them more fundamentally than love – the confrontation with death. Thoughts of death haunt Anna from the time of her first meeting with Vronsky, when he made such questionable use of the fatal accident at the railway station to establish a bond with her. As she grows more darkly convinced that there is no future for their love, and being now pregnant, she remembers a dream she had long before, of a peasant who speaks in French of how the iron must be beaten and pounded (IV, 3): it is not hard to hear ominous overtones here, as she herself does, or recognize this figure again working on the rails where she dies. It was, Tolstoy tells us later – thereby giving a characteristically lifelike twist to his artistic contrivance – a dream she had had often, 'even before her connection with Vronsky'. The rather obvious literary effect produced by such an evidently fateful, even prophetic dream is rendered a good deal more subtle by the psychological realism suggested by the fact that it comes back to her now, and that she should use it to warn Vronsky that she will, and half wishes to, die. When she dreams it again on the night before she dies, the fact of recurrence creates an impression that her doom is embedded in her psyche. Again, the echo awakened in Vronsky's mind of a dream of his own, in which a peasant muttering in French (but for him unintelligibly) had sent a chill down his spine, provides further realistic cover for a similarly obvious parallel (IV, 2). By such touches as these, Tolstoy intensifies the imaginative impression that some fatal necessity, some basic law of life, governs the course of this love story; he typically uses − for Levin, as for Pierre in *War and Peace* − a peasant to communicate his profoundest truths, as though from such a source they are more real than any merely intellectual idea. That both Anna and Vronsky hear a peasant voice which, quite unnaturally, speaks French, and that it comes to them in a nightmare, as it were from the depths of their unconscious, adds an unmistakably sinister note to this utterance from the deep.

For all that Levin is obsessed by the question of what to live for − and his entire seriousness as a person must convince us that his obsession with death is for him (as it was for his author) no mere philosophic speculation but a genuine torment of soul − he to some extent induces this crisis in himself purely by thinking; to transcend it, he has only to trust to his capacity for life, his love for his family, and his openness to the needs of others. Not so Anna; there is no life, there is no one else to sustain her; and so she is utterly consumed by her sense that she must die. This sense is both spiritual and physical; it is as strong as her jealousy, as her sexual vengefulness towards Vronsky, as her entire emotional need for happiness, as her bitterness at losing her son, as her resentment at society; indeed, her sense of fatality is compounded of all these things together, including her addiction to drugs, her doses of morphine and opium. In her case, as in Levin's, Tolstoy reverses the emphasis common amongst naturalist writers, and in fact common amongst his own minor characters. He understands well enough how to belittle ideas, by making them seem to be merely the effect of bodily and material circumstances: for instance, a pleasant kind of self-indulgence in Oblonsky, or a slightly wet kind of emotional and imaginative inadequacy in Koznyshev, or a self-protective flight from a painful reality in Karenin. But with Anna and Levin he enhances their ideas by lending them the full weight of the whole person; in them the body becomes an amplification rather than a reduction. Tolstoy does more than communicate to us Anna's thoughts about death; he makes us share her physical awareness of death, her horror as the candle burns down and she watches the shadows engulf the ceiling. This is no facile symbolism; Anna's shock as the candle goes out seems frighteningly realistic: '"Death!" she thought. And such horror fell upon her that for a long while she could not make out where she was, and her trembling hands could not find a match with which to light another candle' (VII, 26). No other writer has succeeded in imagining his way so far into the subjective experience of dying — and in many powerful passages in other novels besides *Anna Karenina* — yet always with a spiritual dignity which rests firmly upon a deeply sympathetic intuition of just what sensations pass through body and mind.

In her last hours, Anna experiences the world about her with the kind of total moral pessimism and doubt which sometimes invade Levin's mind; she lives his darkest thoughts. Sights and sounds, people and places are penetrated by the same idea: Are we not all flung into the world for no other purpose than to hate each other? Were we not all created in order to suffer, and do we not all know this and all try to invent means for deceiving ourselves? She sees it all distinctly in a glaring light which reveals to her now the utterly negative meaning of life and of human relations. It is from just such despair that Levin is saved — by virtue of the physical and spiritual contentment of his life. At the last the reader may feel that Levin and Anna do not merely contrast but in fact complement one another, and play after all mutually coherent roles as hero and heroine. He is there not simply in order to put her into the wrong, but rather into something like a whole picture of life, which completes and redeems the broken meaning of her own. Her story, on the other hand, provides the novel with a narrative focus which his story, if it is one, does not have; it is no more than a rather

loose assemblage of life's more ordinary incidents. He sur-
mounts his little crises, he does not assert his individuality at
the price of tragedy or even of any very great unhappiness. He
discovers and affirms the more than personal happiness of
life's sameness, the general and abiding life of mankind, the
life whose meaning cannot be individualized into particular
words. Yet just this larger wholeness, this reality beyond
individual tragedy, which Levin senses, is what enables Anna
to become, by contrast, the unique heroine she is. She breaks
all community with others, to realize a condition of utter
separateness, and to assert her own individuality in a gesture
of quite appalling defiance: by destroying the only other
individual who means anything to her at all. The self-
assurance in Vronsky which so irritates her is symbolic of his
separateness, the essence of his individuality, and the very
tragic principle of existence as she sees it. To endure such a
tragic vision of life Tolstoy needed Levin, and Levin's salvation, in order to contain Anna's tragedy, the tragedy of a
world in which there is truly nothing beyond the mutually
destructive claims of individual beings. By the end of the
novel we come to see perhaps what Tolstoy meant by the
opening sentence: 'All happy families are similar to one
another, but each unhappy family is unhappy in its own way.'
No great literature, no very distinctive thought, can be
expected from common happiness or the generality of things;
but each more individual way treads a path of error and conflict and pain. On that waywardness life takes its inescapable
revenge, by virtue of a moral law embedded in the human
psyche and the social structure of experience. Tolstoy's choice
of epigraph prompts us to see that revenge as the vengeance
of God. He is reported to have said of it:

I chose this epigraph to express the idea that whatever is evil,
whatever man does, brings bitter consequences, not from people,
but from God and from what Anna Karenina experiences herself.
(Letter from M. Sukhotin to Veresayev, 23 May 1907)

Chapter 3

The critical context

As successive instalments of *Anna Karenina* appeared in *The Russian Herald* from 1875 onwards, the public greeted them with great excitement and enthusiasm. So, at least, Tolstoy's friend Strakhov reported to him: 'Everyone is taking up your novel. It's incredible how many people are reading it. Only Gogol and Pushkin have been read like this' (? Feb. 1877). Amongst critics there was once again considerable difference of opinion, owing in part to the fact that reviews were often dominated by the political views of the journal for which they were written; they were also written in response to quite short instalments of the text, which may further explain some of the more surprising incomprehension regarding the novel's overall artistic power. There were those who, doubtless with *War and Peace* in mind, thought this a poor sequel, its intellectual hero Levin 'busy not with the freemasons or with Napoleon but with red skewbald cows' (Solovyov, *St Petersburg News*, 1875, no. 65). Even Anna was said to be uninteresting, and Vronsky's unhappiness 'boring . . . the reader expects descriptions of another reality from a writer as talented as Count Tolstoy' (Ibid. no. 105). Another reviewer asked: 'Is it really worth studying this high society which has been exhausted by our so-called upper-class authors and which Count Tolstoy himself does not regard at all favourably?' (Chuyko, *Voice*, 1875, no. 105). To the radical left-wing writer P. N. Tkachov it seemed that 'the creator of *War and Peace* must logically come to writing *Anna Karenina*':

If of the important and remarkable historical events and the notable rise of the people during the first half of the reign of Alexander I Count Tolstoy had such a mystical opinion, in which both those events and that social movement and the participants in it seem nothing but rubbish, then it is natural that the social movements of our time, by no means so remarkable, must remain quite unnoticed, insignificant, and not worthy of the slightest attention. This is just what we have in *Anna Karenina*. Because of his artistic and philosophical theories, the author of the novel sees no interest at all in the general phenomena of life which go beyond the sexual, the personal or the family, and he feeds his creative talents only on the latter, for they alone in his view are the be all and end all of human existence. (*Affair*, 1875, no. 5)

Reviewers with less of a political axe to grind were nevertheless ready to agree with 'the majority of critics that a great talent is being wasted on absolutely insignificant subject-matter, such as the depiction of empty lives, foolish concepts and petty interests' (*Russian News*, 1876, no. 43). There were more jokes about cows, and 'the delightful aroma of babies' nappies', and the remark by the satirical novelist, Saltykov-Shchedrin, that the novel's atmosphere was genito-urinary; and in a letter of 1875 the latter also observed that the conservatives were triumphant; the novel had become their political flag (Knowles, *Tolstoy*, p. 26). Conservative opinion did not so much dispute the details as put a different valuation on them. Avseenko declared that: 'The secret of the fascination which surrounds the novel's heroes and heroines lies precisely in that it retains in itself and its life characteristics of outmoded people of a bygone age, and that it is instinctively and organically opposed to the middle class' (*Russian World*, 1875, no. 69). Above all, of course, it could be said that traditional virtues of domestic life were being vindicated and adultery punished. Only gradually did critics begin to look beyond these topical issues to the artistic and psychological virtues of the text, which have been so much appreciated since. Even Turgenev, who admired 'magnificent pages — the horse race, the mowing, hunting' — was distracted by local, personal associations: 'It is all sour, with an odour of Moscow, incense, spinsterhood, the Slavophile thing and the gentry thing' (Letter, 25 May 1875). By 1879, the novel was being praised (in an American review) as 'a masterpiece without equal in any literature', but still the criticism persisted of 'the moral and social creed of this great poet of the

Russian aristocracy: ". . . be still more indolent, retire once
for all from public life, bury yourselves in your families, on
your estates, and you shall be saved!'" (*North American
Review*, no. 128). Looking back in 1905, Kropotkin recalled:
'The novel produced in Russia a decidedly unfavourable impression, which brought to Tolstoy congratulations from the
reactionary camp and a very cool reception from the advanced portion of society' (*Russian Literature: Ideals and
Realities*).

Eventually even the most advanced circles in Russia learnt
not to let Tolstoy's religious views stand in the way of an appreciation of his art. The clue was given by Lenin in an article
on the occasion of Tolstoy's eightieth birthday: the man and
his work have to be seen as riddled with contradictions, but
contradictions which the thinking of Marx and Engels makes
comprehensible. 'They express the contradictory conditions
of Russian life in the last third of the nineteenth century . . .
The sum total of his views, taken as a whole, happens to express the specific features of our revolution . . .' (*Collected
Works*, XV, 205). No matter, then, that Tolstoy had no
understanding of socialism, and preached religion; the great
realism of his art reveals the social and historical conditions
of emergent capitalism in Russia with its peculiar development towards a peasant – bourgeois revolution. It logically
had to reveal this, since great art mirrors truth, and that is the
Marxist truth about the society Tolstoy depicts. Soviet
criticism has broadly followed this line, and it was expounded
with greater subtlety in 1936 by the Hungarian critic, G.
Lukács. In his observations about *Anna Karenina* he naturally draws attention to the peasant problem, to Levin's confused and unsuccessful attempts to resolve it, to his argument
with Oblonsky, and to the latter's cynical acceptance of the
new economic order. Lukács does not rest his case, however,
primarily on bits of the text which have to do explicitly with
problems of class, ownership, exploitation, and the like.
There would obviously not be enough of them, and he
dismisses this piecemeal approach, which is bound to show
that Tolstoy was interested overwhelmingly in the aristocratic

and landed class, as 'vulgar sociology'. What needs to be understood, Lukács argues, is the artistic basis and structure of Tolstoy's realism, as well as the broader European tradition of realism in fiction and its manner of reflecting social truth. He rests his case − that, despite Tolstoy's reactionary opinions, he did see the true condition of man and society − on the style and form of the novels, rather than on their content (see *Studies in European Realism*, 1950).

The great merit of Lukács's approach is that it places Tolstoy's fiction, with much specific reference to *Anna Karenina*, in a broad historical context of the novel form in Europe and of realism (a subject on which Lukács had published his first major work). He analyses such matters as typicality of characterization, the organization of detail into coherent and living scenes, the scope for action within a realistic modern milieu, the relationship of characters to their background, the treatment of their inner world, and so on − matters which are fundamental and largely unique to the form of the novel. And he argues on each point that Tolstoy maintains through his style of fiction that vision of the world which distinguishes the 'great realists' of the early nineteenth century, Stendhal and Balzac. Each point is further sharpened by the contrast Lukács draws with Tolstoy's contemporaries in France and Germany, realists whom he noticeably calls modern rather than great. In Flaubert, Zola, and Maupassant the realist vision fails: character becomes mediocre, action banal, detail trivial, background tawdry and inhuman. These writers are mere detached observers of their material; they do not participate in it morally and imaginatively, as Tolstoy so preeminently does. The so-called naturalism of the new realists is quite unnatural in the alienation it implies of man from his environment; the contrived poeticism of its style is itself consciously alienated from any real poetry in things. Both these considerations provide further obvious contrast with Tolstoy, who can still conceive of man living in idyllic harmony with his surroundings in a way which goes back to the epic life of Homer's time. Tolstoy knew such harmony was precarious, and the spiritual crisis which overcame him soon after writing *Anna Karenina* (Lukács interprets it as in essence social rather than religious) made further such writing impossible. However, although Tolstoy's increasingly radical attitudes recommended him to the new generation of naturalists and expressionists, his great humane realism was never quite extinguished. And in this he resembles Ibsen, with whom Lukács further compares him: another giant who was able to preserve an older and profounder wisdom against the bleakness of modernity — thanks to his exceptional social situation, Lukács always notes, though this explanation scarcely adds very much to his literary perceptions.

Many critics, of course, have brought out the distinctiveness of *Anna Karenina* by means of comparisons with other novels. Matthew Arnold thought it 'very advantageously distinguished from the type of novel now so much in request in France' (*Essays in Criticism*, second series, 1886). In particular, by contrast with *Madame Bovary*, he found no 'lubricity', nor any of the 'cruelty of petrified feeling' with which Flaubert pursues his heroine 'without pity or cause'. Arnold repeatedly stresses not only how lifelike, but also how likeable Anna is. 'Throughout her course, with its failures, errors, and miseries, the impression of her large, fresh, rich, generous, delightful nature never leaves us — keeps our sympathy, keeps even, I had almost said, our respect'. He seems to reproach himself for feeling that 'Count Tolstoy's heroines are really so living and charming that one takes them, fiction though they are, too seriously.' He excuses himself for being so English as to register surprise that Anna yields to her passion without struggle, before yielding himself to 'the triumph of Anna's charm that . . . remains paramount nevertheless'. In a similar spirit he notes that there are too many incidents and too many characters in the novel, 'if we look in it for a work of art in which the action shall be vigorously one, and to that one action everything shall converge'. He simply abandons rather than answers this objection, happily untroubled by any theoretical concern about the nature of realism: 'The truth is we are not to take *Anna Karénine* as a work of art; we are to take it as a piece of life.'

The most celebrated phrase regarding Tolstoy's artlessness and the view that 'such things are "superior to art"' was coined by Henry James. He was thinking primarily of *War and Peace*, along with Thackeray's *The Newcomes* and *Les Trois Mousquetaires*, and he asked: 'What do such large loose baggy monsters, with their queer elements of the accidental and the arbitrary, artistically *mean*?' (*The Tragic Muse*, Preface, 1907–9). George Sainstbury was ready enough to explain in his contemptuous diatribe against Tolstoy:' "Pieces of life" perhaps they are, but in a strangely unlicked and unfinished condition.' The result was sheer crudity, and he pronounced Anna's 'false love' to be 'infinitely less interesting than that of Emma Bovary' (*Periods of European Literature*, XII, 1907). Another critic to contrast this aspect of *Anna Karenina* more subtly but still unfavourably with the more formal conventions of the novel in France was Percy Lubbock. He notes the rapidity of Anna's fall: 'Anna is in the midst of her crisis and has passed it before it is possible to know her life clearly from within.' Lubbock rather convincingly imagines how Balzac would have proceeded: 'He would have been too busy with his prodigious summary of the history and household of the Karenins to permit himself a glance in the direction of any particular moment.' And he judges Tolstoy's method to be faulty: 'His refusal to shape his story . . . prevents him from making the most of the space at his command.' Lubbock concludes that the reader cannot see consequently how Vronsky comes to mean so much to Anna; he is Tolstoy's 'one failure . . . a failure not with him, but with her, in the prelude of the book' (*The Craft of Fiction*, 1921). Perhaps the best revision of these critical concepts, from the formal methods associated with realism to the impression of life given by Tolstoy's departure from them, is that undertaken by John Bayley in *Tolstoy and the Novel* (1966). He reinterprets the difference between Tolstoy and Balzac, and discovers the artistic meaning of the 'episodic method' which James could not. Yet he too admits that Tolstoy attempted 'with less success to retain it in *Anna Karenina*, whose situation and story are strictly comparable with a novel of Western realism. We cannot but help think of Anna in the context of such a novel, and so our ignorance about her upbringing and background are not an unmixed advantage.'

Many critics have been impressed less by 'elements of the arbitrary and accidental' in *Anna Karenina* than by the novel's vital unity and coherence, and have accordingly looked for other connective threads in the style. K. Leontiev did this already in 1890 (in his untranslated 'Analysis, Style, and Trend'), and more recently, since the work of R. Jakobson (*Fundamentals of Language*, 1956, 78) and the third volume of Eykhenbaum's major study (1960), patterns of symbolism have been widely explored. These and other forms of structural linkage are well laid out, to reveal the 'functional value' of many a supposed digression, in E. Stenbock-Fermor's *Architecture of 'Anna Karenina'*, 1975, and again by S. Schultze in *The Structure of 'Anna Karenina'*, 1982. Most recent critics have in fact drawn attention to the artistic organization of the novel: R. F. Christian, for instance, in his *Critical Introduction*, 1969, and Logan Speirs, who has a chapter on 'The Structuring of *Anna Karenina*' (*Tolstoy and Chekhov, 1971*).

Yet there are likely to be many readers still for whom the tremendous life and strength of the novel are best accounted for in moral terms, and doubtless Tolstoy himself would have approved of this, although not of all that has been written on this score. The difficulty of determining the moral meaning of *Anna Karenina* has given rise to a wider range of views than the elusive artistic meaning of its various parts. When E.-M. de Vogüé recommended the superior spiritual qualities of the Russian novelists to the cynical and materialist generation of his contemporaries in France (*Le Roman russe*, 1886), he found in Tolstoy less of 'Christian charity' or 'social pity' than in Gogol, Turgenev, or Dostoyevsky. Instead, he encountered 'something occult and fearful, the ever-present shadow of the Infinite . . . a question silenced by the Inaccessible, a far-away sigh breathed by Fate over Nothingness'. L. I. Shestov was so impressed by Tolstoy's ability to 'push Anna Karenina under a train and not to utter a sigh', and by similar examples of pitilessness in his fiction, that he wrote a book comparing the conception of 'Good in the Teaching of Tolstoy and Nietzsche' (1900). He believed that Tolstoy urges us to 'seek for that which is *above* pity, *above* Good. We must seek for God.' The implications of the novel's epigraph can sound exceedingly grim, but others have questioned this: J. P Stern, for instance, in his comparison of fatality in *Anna Karenina*, *Madame Bovary*, and *Effi Briest* (*Re-interpretations*, 1964). D. S. Merezhkovsky stressed at least the degree of 'mechanical' sympathy, of almost physical participation, which Tolstoy's prose arouses by its unparalleled evocation of the bodily reality of the characters and of their experiences; he called Tolstoy a 'seer of the flesh' (*Tolstoy and Dostoyevsky*, 1901). Better known in England perhaps is Lawrence's praise for Tolstoy's 'marvellous sensuous understanding' which owes its power to his vision, shared with Shakespeare, Sophocles, and Hardy, of 'the vast, uncomprehended and incomprehensible morality of nature or of life itself, surpassing human consciousness'. Lawrence comprehended this 'greater unwritten morality' well enough for him to feel that Anna and Vronsky had been unfaithful to it — or rather that Tolstoy had been — in allowing mere conventional human morality to triumph. This attractive but untenable view roused F. R. Leavis to a rather rare disagreement with Lawrence (*Anna Karenina and Other Essays*, 1967), while the point at issue, less extravagantly formulated, has led to some of the most interesting moral debate about the novel (see H. Gifford, *Leo Tolstoy, A Critical Anthology*, 1971).

Guide to further reading

Editions of Tolstoy's works in Russian

Polnoye sobraniye sochinenii ed, V. G. Chertkov *et al.*, 90 vols., Moscow, 1928–58 (The Jubilee Edition).
Sobraniye sochineni, 20 vols., Moscow, 1960–5.

Editions in English

Works, tr. L. and A. Maude, 21 vols., Oxford, 1928–37 (The Centenary Edition, available in The World's Classics).
Complete Works, tr. Leo Wiener, 24 vols., Boston and London, 1904–5.
New Light on Tolstoy, Literary Fragments etc., tr. P. England, ed. R. Fülöp-Miller, New York and London, 1931.
Individual works are available in the Everyman Library and in Penguin Translations.
Letters, selected, ed. and tr. R. F. Christian, 2 vols., London, 1978.
Tolstoy's Diaries, ed, and tr. R. F. Christian, 2 vols., London, 1985.

Biographical studies

Mann, T., 'Goethe and Tolstoy', in *Essays of Three Decades*, tr. H. T. Lowe-Porter, London, 1947.
Maude, A., *The Life of Tolstoy*, 2 vols., Oxford, 1930 (in the Centenary Edition).
Rolland, R., *Tolstoy*, tr. B. Miall, London, 1911.
Simmons, E. J., *Leo Tolstoy*, London 1946.
Troyat, H., *Tolstoy*, tr. N. Amphoux, London, 1968.

There are many books of reminiscences of Tolstoy by his family and contemporaries: for instance, *The Diary of Tolstoy's Wife*, tr. S. A. Werth, London, 1928; *The Autobiography of Countess Sophie Tolstoy*, tr. S. S. Koteliansky and L. Woolf, London, 1922; *Family Views of Tolstoy*, tr. L. and A. Maude, London 1926; and memoirs by three of his sons.

Critical studies

Bayley, J., *Tolstoy and the Novel*, London, 1966.

Berlin, Isaiah, *The Hedgehog and the Fox*, New York and London, 1953.

Christian, R. F., *Tolstoy: A Critical Introduction*, Cambridge, 1969.

Eykhenbaum, B. M., *Lev Tolstoy*, 3 vols., Leningrad, 1928; Moscow, 1931, Leningrad, 1960; vol. I, *The Young Tolstoy*, tr. G. Kern, Ann Arbor, 1972.

Gifford, Henry, *Tolstoy*, Oxford, 1982.

Greenwood, E. B., *Tolstoy: The Comprehensive Vision*, London, 1975.

Jones, Malcolm (ed.), *New Essays on Tolstoy*, Cambridge, 1978.

Knowles, A. V., *Tolstoy, The Critical Heritage*, London, 1978.

Leavis, F. R., *Anna Karenina and Other Essays*, London, 1967.

Lukács, G., *Studies in European Realism*, ch. VI, tr. E. Bone, London, 1950.

Matlaw, Ralph E. (ed.), *Tolstoy: A Collection of Critical Essays*, Englewood Cliffs, N.J., 1967.

Redpath, Theodore, *Tolstoy*, London, 1960.

Schultze, Sydney, *The Structure of 'Anna Karenina'*, Ann Arbor, 1982.

Simmons, E. J., *An Introduction to Tolstoy's Writings*, Chicago, 1968.

Speirs, Logan, *Tolstoy and Chekhov*, Cambridge, 1971.

Spence, G. W., *Tolstoy the Ascetic*, Edinburgh and London, 1967.

Steiner, G., *Tolstoy or Dostoyevsky: An Essay in Contrast*, rev. ed. Harmondsworth, 1967.

Stenbock-Fermor, E., *The Architecture of 'Anna Karenina'*, Louvain, 1975.

Wasiolek, E., *Tolstoy's Major Fiction*, Chicago and London, 1978.

Zhdanov, V. A., *Tvorcheskaya istoriya Anny Kareninoy*, Moscow, 1957; *Ot 'Anny Kareninoy' k 'Voskreseniyu'* Moscow, 1967.